Leo Tolstoy

Twayne's World Authors Series
Russian Literature

Charles A. Moser, Editor
George Washington University

TWAS 772

LEO TOLSTOY
(1828–1910)
Photograph, 1868

Leo Tolstoy

By William W. Rowe

George Washington University

Twayne Publishers • Boston

Leo Tolstoy

William W. Rowe

Copyright © 1986 by G. K. Hall & Co.
All Rights Reserved
Published by Twayne Publishers
A Division of G. K. Hall & Co.
70 Lincoln Street
Boston, Massachusetts 02111

Copyediting supervised by Lewis DeSimone
Book production by Elizabeth Todesco
Book design by Barbara Anderson

Typeset in 11 pt. Garamond
by Compset, Inc., Beverly, Massachusetts

Printed on permanent/durable acid-free paper
and bound in the United States of America

Library of Congress Cataloging in Publication Data

Rowe, William Woodin.
  Leo Tolstoy.

  (Twayne's world authors series. Russian literature; TWAS 772)
  Bibliography: p. 137
  Includes index.
  1. Tolstoy, Leo, graf, 1828–1910—Criticism and
interpretation.   I. Title.   II. Series.
PG3410.R69   1986   891.73'3   85-22013
ISBN 0-8057-6623-5

For Eleanor

Contents

About the Author

W. W. Rowe was born in New York City and took his undergraduate degree at Harvard. He received his Ph.D. in 1968 from New York University and has taught at the George Washington University in Washington, D.C., where he is currently professor of Russian, since 1970.

Rowe's principal interests are nineteenth-century Russian literature and the works of Vladimir Nabokov. He is the author of *Dostoevsky: Child and Man in His Works* (1968), *Nabokov's Deceptive World* (1971), *Through Gogol's Looking Glass: Reverse Vision, False Focus and Precarious Logic* (1976), *Nabokov and Others: Patterns in Russian Literature* (1979), and *Nabokov's Spectral Dimension* (1981).

Preface

To do justice within the sensible confines of a Twayne book to a person whose complete collected works number ninety volumes is no easy task. It was impossible to cover all of Tolstoy's writings in depth, as it was to acknowledge fully all the valuable critical commentaries devoted to these writings. My primary aim has been to present a picture of Tolstoy the man, thinker, and writer, as well as to offer careful readings of *War and Peace, Anna Karenina, Resurrection,* and some of his more important shorter works.

Writing about reading Tolstoy, Yury Olesha has suggested that just as there are scientific miracles, so there are "miracles of literature." As an example, he cites Tolstoy's description of the night sky in one of his Caucasian stories. It would be worthwhile, Olesha declares, to collect a hundred such miracles in order to demonstrate how some people can think and see: "even those who cannot so think and see would respect themselves at that moment, understanding that inasmuch as they are also people, they are capable of much."[1] I have tried, in the pages that follow, to collect some Tolstoyan miracles, to make them available to the English reader, and to relate their individual spendor to the overall pattern of his art.

The final chapter seeks—incautiously but I hope usefully—to describe the awesome scope of Tolstoy's vision, his views on the place, purpose, and potential of human beings, and the essence of his lasting greatness as an artist. Translations of Tolstoy's literary works are my own. Textual references are to the current twenty-two volume Soviet edition of Tolstoy's writings: *Sobranie sochinenii v dvadtsati dvukh tomakh* (Moscow: Khudozhestvennaia literatura, 1978–). Publication of this edition has now reached volume seventeen.

I am grateful to Charles Moser, the editor of this series, for his numerous valuable suggestions and to my wife, Eleanor, for her essential insights and support. Of course, I alone am responsible for any errors or misreadings in this study.

William W. Rowe

George Washington University

Chronology

1880–1881   *A Criticism of Dogmatic Theory* and *A Translation and Harmony of the Four Gospels*. Both are banned.

1883   Meets V. G. Chertkov.

1884   *What I Believe* is banned.

1885   "What People Live By." Helps Chertkov establish Intermediary publishing house, to make good literature widely available at low cost. Rift with wife widens.

1886   "The Death of Ivan Ilych" and "How Much Land Does A Man Need?" Writes *The Power of Darkness*.

1888   Thirteenth and last child born. "Strider."

1889   Begins *Resurrection*.

1890   *The Kreutzer Sonata* is banned.

1891–1892   Renounces rights to works published after 1881. Organizes famine relief.

1893   Finishes *The Kingdom of God Is Within You*.

1894–1895   "Master and Man." Visited by Bunin and Chekhov.

1897   Completes *What Is Art?*

1898   Organizes aid for Dukhobors.

1899   *Resurrection*.

1901   Excommunicated from the Orthodox Church. "Reply to the Holy Synod's Edict." Moves to the Crimea because of health. Visited by Gorky.

1902–1903   Writes to Nicholas II urging social reforms and warning of possible rebellion. Protests Jewish pogroms in Kishinyov.

1905–1906   Writes several stories (all published posthumously) and an afterword to Chekhov's "The Darling." Wife seriously ill. Favorite daughter dies.

1907–1908   Writes to Prime Minister Stolypin, advocating abolition of private property. Publishes *I Cannot Be Silent* (against capital punishment).

1910   Leaves home. Falls ill and dies on 7 November at Astapovo railway station. Buried at Yasnaya Polyana.

Chapter One

Biography

Childhood and Youth, 1828–51

The name *Leo* approximates *Lev* ("lion" in Russian), but "giant" might seem more appropriate. When Leo Tolstoy died in 1910, he was known as "the second Tsar of Russia," beloved by all classes and admired throughout the world. His prodigious artistic creations had established him as one of the literary giants of his age: no man of letters since Voltaire had achieved such prominence. By his boldly proclaimed moral and spiritual teachings he had become the foremost voice of conscience and religion in his time. Leo Tolstoy seemed to tower over Russia, shaking the foundations of its governmental and religious institutions. Among the countless people he influenced was Gandhi, who once referred to himself as "a humble follower" of Tolstoy's.

Tolstoy continually searched for an answer to the question: "What is the aim of human life?"[1] With the all-observant eye of genius he recorded what was, even as he sought to promote his passionate vision of what ought to be. Tolstoy combined, in Isaiah Berlin's famous formulation, a "fox-like" ability to maintain diverse views with a "hedgehog-like" effort to discover the "One Truth."[2] In his moral and spiritual quest, he sometimes conscientiously reasoned his way to extremes. Tolstoy's fiction, which is quite autobiographical, reflects this quest.

Leo was born on 28 August 1828, at Yasnaya Polyana ("clear glade"), about 130 miles south-west of Moscow. This estate had belonged to his mother's family, the Volkonskys, who were allegedly descended from Rurik, founder of the Kievan dynasty. Grandfather Nikolay Volkonsky (1753–1821) was a stern landowner but provided wisely and generously for his serfs. He loved his daughter Marya, whose mother had died when the girl was two, and strictly taught her geometry and physics. Above his piercing eyes, he had bushy, jutting eyebrows, which his grandson Leo inherited. Marya herself was rather plain-looking, and had virtually given up all hope of marriage when, at thirty-two, she met Nikolay Tolstoy.

The Tolstoys go back to a certain Indris, probably a Lithuanian

knight who came to Russia in 1353. Leo's great-great-great grandfather Peter lived during the reign of Peter the Great. A ruthless oppor-
tunist, he led a generally successful life until implicated in the murder
of Aleksey, the heir to the throne, in 1718. He died in prison, but his
grandson Andrey, an administrative official, restored the family's
wealth and prominence. The Empress Elizabeth conferred upon him
the title of count, and his wife bore him twenty-three children, one of
whom, Ilya Tolstoy (1757–1820), was Leo's grandfather. Foolishly
generous and prodigal, Ilya would have his sturgeon shipped in from
Astrakhan and his laundry done in Holland, and thus squandered the
family fortunes. His son Nikolay Tolstoy (1795–1837) received his
sexual initiation at the age of sixteen with a servant girl as arranged by
his parents. At eighteen, he served in the army when Napoleon invad-
ed Russia. After his father died in 1820, Nikolay had to make a marriage of convenience to restore the family's depleted finances. Nikolay
had the Tolstoy name and important connections; the unglamorous
Marya Volkonskaya brought to the marriage in 1822 the estate of Yasnaya Polyana and its eight hundred serfs.

During the first six years of her marriage, Marya gave birth to four
sons—Nikolay, Sergey, Dmitry, and Leo—and died in 1830, not long
after giving birth to a daughter, Marya, when Leo was almost two. The
children took turns spending the night with their grandmother, Pelageya Tolstaya, who died in 1838. Leo's deeply religious aunt, Alexandra Tolstaya, also lived at Yasnaya Polyana, as did "Auntie" Tatyana,
his father's second cousin, who had a profound influence upon Leo and
advised him to write novels.[3] This gentle, affectionate person, he later
recalled, taught him from a very early age "the spiritual delight of
love."[4] When he was five, Leo was moved downstairs to live with his
older brothers and their exacting but kindly German tutor. He was
such a sensitive child that he soon was given the nickname "Leo Cry-
Baby" (*Lyova Ryova*).

Painfully concerned about what others thought of him, Leo imitated
his self-assured brother Sergey, but it was Nikolay who fired his imagination. Nikolay told his younger brothers many fantastic stories, and
one day announced that there existed a secret through which all men
could become "Ant Brothers" and live in perfect health and harmony.
The secret, he said, was written on a little green stick buried in a
nearby forest. Even though the word "Ant" probably derived from a
confusion between "Moravian" and *muravei* ("ant" in Russian), more

than sixty-five years later Tolstoy would insist that he still believed in the existence of such a world-saving Truth.[5]

When Leo was eight, the children were taken to Moscow to be educated more thoroughly. A few months later their father died suddenly, and Leo, who had not seen the body, kept stubbornly hoping to meet him on the street. His grandmother then died within a year, and although the boy found some relief in playing the role of aggrieved orphan, he was deeply pained by the inevitability of death. Attitudes toward death, as well as rather moralistic descriptions of moribund states of mind and heart, would become a major theme in Tolstoy's novels and stories.

Leo's devout Aunt Alexandra now become the children's legal guardian, and a new tutor, Saint-Thomas, took over their education. Though a capable teacher, he disastrously offended Leo by threatening to flog him. Humiliated and indignant, the boy imagined dramatic scenarios of triumph over his enemy and developed an early aversion to cruelty and violence. Saint-Thomas soon changed his tactics and began to flatter Leo, whose vanity was to be a source of self-dissatisfaction for much of his life.

Though not an outstanding student, Leo pursued a wide variety of ideas with remarkable intensity for a boy of eleven or twelve. He thought deeply about the concept of eternity and the possibility of reincarnation. In order to develop self-discipline and endurance, he would whip his bare back and hold a heavy book at arm's length for as long as five minutes. A keen awareness of the inevitability of death would then lead him to devour sweets and sink into lethargy for several days. In *Otrochestvo* (*Boyhood*), he later described his practice of whirling around suddenly to "catch emptiness unawares"—because external objects, owing their existence to his consciousness, had presumably vanished when he stopped paying attention to them.

Aunt Alexandra died in the summer of 1841, and Leo, barely thirteen, moved to Kazan to live with her sister Pelageya Yushkova. There, Leo sadly concluded that his unruly hair, wide nose, and thick lips made him unattractive. His shyness intensified, and he developed rules for being comme il faut in social situations. This period also saw the awakening of an intense sexual desire that would cause problems for most of his life. At fourteen, Leo was excited by one of the Yushkovs' maids. When he was just sixteen, his brothers took him to a brothel; after losing his virginity (he recalled much later), he stood beside the prostitute's bed and wept. He also dreamed of a beautiful, ideal woman who would unite with him in perfect happiness.

Planning to become a diplomat, Leo studied to enter the Department of Oriental Languages at the University of Kazan. He failed parts of his entrance examination in the spring of 1844, but retook them in the fall and passed. The next summer he decided to study law and sought to follow his "Rules of Life"—a demanding program of mental and physical self-improvement. He did strenuous exercises designed to make him "the strongest man in the world,"[6] and read voraciously: Russian classics, French novels, Charles Dickens (*David Copperfield*), the New Testament (especially Matthew), Georg Wilhelm Friedrich Hegel, and François Voltaire. He revered Jean-Jacques Rousseau, who reinforced his developing belief in the sanctity of the natural life. Still, Leo was doing rather poorly in his second year of law study; now nearly nineteen, he was about to gain legal control of Yasnaya Polyana. He had recently contracted gonorrhea, as his diary of 1847 reveals, so he successfully petitioned to leave the university for what he termed "ill health and domestic circumstances."

At Yasnaya Polyana in 1847–48, Tolstoy attempted to improve his estate and ameliorate the lot of his peasants: his well-meaning but naive efforts encountered laziness, cynical suspicion, and perplexing resignation. Moreover, his rules for self-improvement were soon forgotten during dissolute sprees in Moscow and St. Petersburg. Tolstoy developed a passion for gambling, which more than once was to bring him close to financial ruin. He now formulated three goals: (1) gamble; (2) marry advantageously; (3) obtain a good post. Returning to Yasnaya Polyana, however, he opened a school for peasant children and studied music. Despite a rigorous exercise routine, he sank deeper into debauchery and thus desperately poured his energy into writing. By January of 1851, his diary recorded the intention to write about his childhood. Still plagued by "voluptuous desires," however, he set off in May for the Caucasus to seek diversion and adventure.

Fame and Marriage, 1851–73

On 30 May 1851, Tolstoy and his older brother Nikolay, a lieutenant, arrived at the Cossack village of Starogladkovskaya. Georgia had become part of the Russian Empire in 1801, and the Russians were still trying to conquer the savage tribes who lived between Georgia and the Terek River. Tolstoy volunteered for action and fought bravely on several occasions. He became the *kunak* (something like "friend to the death") of a young native named Sado, who then won back a large gambling-debt I.O.U. of Tolstoy's just before it fell due. Tolstoy, who had prayed for help the night before, viewed this as divine intervention. He struck up another close friendship with a white-haired, Herculean hedonist named Daddy Epishka, who assured his young friend that love was not a sin but a salvation.

Tolstoy soon wrote to Auntie Tatyana that he had come down with "a kind of hot fever," but in a letter to Nikolay he complained that the mercury which cured his venereal disease had painful after-effects. During his convalescence, Tolstoy completed the first part of *Detstvo* (*Childhood*). On 3 July 1852, he sent the manuscript, signed only with the initials L. N., to Nikolay Nekrasov, editor of the journal *Sovremennik* (the *Contemporary*). "L. N." requested that the manuscript be considered for publication and explained that it was the beginning of a four-part novel. Nekrasov published it, considerably edited, under the title *A History of My Childhood*. Tolstoy objected to these changes, but his anger was soon assuaged by the acclaim that greeted his work, including praise from Turgenev and Dostoevsky.

During the Crimean War of 1853–56 Tolstoy obtained a transfer to Sevastopol, where he fought in the famous Fourth Bastion during the heavy siege of that city in the spring of 1855. After Sevastopol had fallen, he left the army to find that he had become a literary hero, having published, in addition to *Boyhood* and "Nabeg" ("The Raid," 1853), his three *Sevastopol'skie rasskazy* (*Sevastopol Stories,* 1855–56). Despite numerous alterations by the censor, the last two of these realistic war tales spoke of cowardice, greed for glory, and the senseless tragedy of military combat. The first one, however, in which Tolstoy praised the noble simplicity and steadfastness of the Russian soldier, had earned him fervent admiration. Alexander II was deeply moved by it, and is said to have given orders to protect the life of the young author.

Arriving in St. Petersburg, Tolstoy stayed with Turgenev, who was at first delighted with his guest, although he called him "the troglodyte" because of his crude enthusiasm and stubbornness and was rather shocked by his nightly sprees. The *Sovremennik* circle also greeted him warmly. However, Tolstoy's outspoken and occasionally perverse opinions soon antagonized both the aristocratic liberals—led by Turgenev—and the radicals, including Nikolay Chernyshevsky. In 1850, Tolstoy's diary had formulated his social goals of choosing difficult positions and dominating conversations; and now he disparaged everyone's favorite writers from George Sand to Shakespeare, quarreling especially often with Turgenev. He did, however, form a permanent friendship with the poet Afanasy Fet.

Early in 1856, Tolstoy was distressed to learn that his brother Dmitry had died of tuberculosis on 21 January. He had recently visited Dmitry, whose gaunt appearance and morose, questioning look deeply depressed him. In May, Tolstoy returned to Yasnaya Polyana convinced that it was time to marry, and commenced a complicated courtship of Valerya Arseneva. For several months, his diary recorded fluctuations between faint revulsion ("she's like noodles") and near ardor ("Do I love her?"), but his attraction weakened decisively when she took offense at his preachments on self-improvement.

In 1857 Tolstoy traveled in western Europe, though his delight in Paris turned to horror when he witnessed a guillotine execution. This "ingenious and elegant machine," he wrote to a friend, is somehow more revolting than tearing a man to pieces.[7] Tolstoy soon left for Switzerland, where he developed an intimate friendship with Countess Alexandra Tolstaya (the daughter of his grandfather's brother), a maid of honor at the Imperial Court of Russia whose influence was to prove crucial on several occasions.

During the next few years Tolstoy devoted much time to his school for peasant children. In 1860 he again traveled to Europe, where he was profoundly shaken by the death of his brother Nikolay—"literally in my arms," he wrote in a gloomy letter to Fet.[8] Early in 1861, Tolstoy was appointed an arbiter of the peace to settle disputes between newly emancipated peasants and their former masters. At Fet's estate he had a bitter quarrel with Turgenev, which almost resulted in a duel. In July of 1862, the police searched the school at Yasnaya Polyana for evidence of subversive activity, an event which elicited an indignant protest from Tolstoy directly to Alexander II. The Countess Alexandra Tolstaya, who had encouraged him to write to the emperor, used her influence at court, and Tolstoy was officially exonerated.

That summer, at the age of thirty-four, Tolstoy fell in love with Sofya Andreevna Behrs (Sonya), who was living with her parents and two sisters on their nearby estate. Sonya was a spirited girl of eighteen with dark hair, large brown eyes, and a sentimental, moody disposition. As a child, she had reverently memorized whole passages from *Childhood* and *Boyhood*. At first the family thought Tolstoy was courting the eldest sister Liza, but one evening he conveyed to Sonya that this was not so: she almost miraculously managed to interpret his explanation when he wrote only the first letters of the words on a card table with chalk. She then composed a story about a girl like herself who loved an unattractive, middle-aged man, the deciphering of which both encouraged and disturbed Tolstoy. After carrying around a written proposal for several days, he resolved to test fate by delivering it only if Sonya's younger sister Tanya sang the end of a particular song well—which she did. Running to her room, Sonya feverishly scanned the letter, which said in part:

Tell me as an *honest woman*—do you wish to be my wife? Only say *yes* if you can do so *fearlessly,* with all your heart. . . . It will be terrible for me to hear "no," but I foresee it. . . .[9]

Although Liza insisted that Sonya refuse, she rushed to Tolstoy and accepted his proposal. They were married on 23 September 1862, after she had read, at his grimly honest insistence, the vivid diary accounts of his former dissolute life.

At first, harmony and joy prevailed: "I didn't know it was possible to be so much in love and so happy," Tolstoy wrote to Countess Alexandra.[10] But there were also quarrels, in part because Sonya, after reading her husband's diary, knew that Aksinya, his most recent mistress, still lived on the estate. In January of 1863 Sonya recorded in her diary a dream wherein she seized Aksinya's child and tore it to pieces—only to realize, as Leo appeared, that the child had been merely a doll. Two months later, in a joint letter to Sonya's sister Tanya, Tolstoy declared that his wife had become a cold china doll. The doll, he wrote, had an unnatural, conelike belly (Sonya was then more than five months pregnant), and he concluded that despite all this, they were happy. On the basis of Tolstoy's diary, Boris Eikhenbaum has suggested that this was written for Sonya—although she may never have interpreted it correctly—as an apology for difficulties in their marital relations.[11]

On 28 June Sonya's first child (of thirteen) was born and christened Sergey. During that year Tolstoy not only published *Kazaki* (*The Cossacks*) and the peasant story "Polikushka," but began to write *Voina i mir* (*War and Peace*). Sonya was initially disappointed when her new husband shut himself up in his study to work on his historical novel, but soon made herself indispensable as she produced clear copies of Tolstoy's nearly indecipherable manuscript. Due to his constant revisions, she copied much of it six or seven times. Her impish sister Tanya, sixteen, visited them and became the inspiration for Natasha

Rostova, the novel's heroine. In October of 1864 Sonya gave birth to a daughter, Tanya. After the first part of Tolstoy's novel appeared in *Russkii vestnik* (the *Russian Messenger*) early in 1865 and after much historical research, he became fascinated by the idea of focusing upon Alexander I and Napoleon. During the next two years, he often discussed the philosophy of history with Moscow friends including the historian Mikhail Pogodin. Meanwhile, Sonya valiantly copied out numerous drafts and corrections. Tolstoy labored so intensely that he suffered from dizziness, but by the end of 1867 he had published the first three volumes in book form. The last three came out in 1868–69, and two more sons, Ilya and Leo, were born. Critical reaction to the novel was generally favorable. Tolstoy's friend Fet and others extolled it. Turgenev at first thought it "boring," but when more of the novel appeared, he praised its "life, truth and freshness." Negative criticism came mainly from those who objected to the explicit assumption that historical events are predetermined, rather than shaped by rulers and leaders.

Tolstoy's six-year effort had been gratifying, but it took its toll. Like Sonya, he was given to fits of unreasonable jealousy and—especially toward the end of this period—to sudden outbursts of anger. In addition, Tolstoy had two very disturbing experiences during these years. In 1866, he attempted to defend a soldier who had been provoked into striking a sadistic officer. Despite Tolstoy's carefully reasoned defense (based on temporary insanity), the soldier was sentenced to be shot. Tolstoy described the other incident, which occurred in 1869 in the town of Arzamas, in the autobiographical tale "Zapiski sumasshedshego" ("Memoirs of a Madman") more than a decade later. Attempting to fall asleep, he was overcome by a strange need to escape from an unknown force. His eerie helplessness was climaxed by what seemed to be the presence of death. Prayers did not help, and Tolstoy was forced to wake up his servant and leave, still haunted by that terrifying experience.

Though close to a breakdown, Tolstoy continued to read extensively and to work on various pedagogical projects. Late in 1869 he read both Kant and Schopenhauer, declaring the latter "the most brilliant of men."[12] He also read Shakespeare, Goethe, and Molière. Tolstoy's writing plans for 1870 yielded to a feverish study of Greek: within three months, he was reading Plato and Homer in the original. Early in 1871 Sonya gave birth to a daughter, Marya. In the fall, Tolstoy compiled what he termed a "primer" for peasant children—essentially a complete curriculum including science, math, and various stories, many of which he wrote.

Crisis and Confession, 1873–90

Tolstoy's spiritual crisis, traditionally dated in the later 1870s, had developed slowly for much of his life, and its progress can be discerned in his mounting dissatisfaction with *Anna Karenina*. As this novel, begun in March of 1873, took shape, he found its focus on adultery deeply displeasing. Returning to pedagogy, he elaborated his educational theories before the Moscow Committee on Literacy and published an article on education in 1874. Almost a decade earlier, Tolstoy had written to Countess Alexandra, expressing a rather Dostoevskian belief in the innate wisdom of the child; he now wrote to her again, declaring that children's "spiritual qualities" were perishing in the schools.[13] His *New Primer* plus four children's readers appeared early in 1875, and he even planned to open a "university in bast shoes" to train peasant teachers, but too few candidates applied.

Tolstoy continued to struggle with his great novel of doomed adultery. "My God, if only someone would finish *Anna Karenina* for me!" he wrote to the critic Nikolay Strakhov in November of 1875. "It's unbearably repulsive."[14] Tolstoy did finish the novel in 1877, and it was immensely popular: Dostoevsky even claimed that there was nothing in European literature that could compare with it. Tolstoy's own family situation, however, had been deteriorating. Auntie Tatyana died in June of 1874, and early in 1875 his baby son Nikolay died of "water on the brain, and after 3 weeks' terrible torture," Tolstoy wrote to Fet.[15] A daughter born prematurely at the end of that year died almost immediately. In 1877 and 1879 two more children were born; Sonya, suffering from poor health and strained nerves, displayed her former jealousy. Worst of all, Tolstoy entered a period of painful spiritual crisis.

Now, at fifty, Tolstoy finally confronted a question that had stalked him for so long: What is the point of life? Death, which had recently struck his family repeatedly, seemed an inescapable, all-erasing reality. If that were so, why not commit suicide? Plagued by an urge to end his own life, Tolstoy made serious efforts to avoid guns, ropes, and other potential temptations. His *Ispoved'* (*Confession*), mostly written by 1880, chronicles his search for a way out of his dilemma. Extensive reading in the sciences uncovered no solutions; a study of philosophy left him with the unhelpful notion that our earthly life is illusory. The people of his social class seemed to have no satisfactory answers. Tolstoy then made a thorough study of religions, including Buddhism and Muhammadanism, which still left his mind unsatisfied. Turning to the peasants, Tolstoy realized that their faith in God provided a possible answer, albeit one not formulated in intellectual terms. He talked with simple, uneducated peasants and pilgrims; he visited monasteries. Realizing that faith gave meaning to these people's lives, Tolstoy overcame his objections and attended Russian Orthodox services. The ceremony soon repelled him, however: he found it particularly hypocritical to pretend that communion wine was the blood of the Lord, and he rejected the Orthodox view that all other beliefs were heretical. In the end, Tolstoy derived the greatest hope from the humble, hardworking, and natural life of Russian peasants.

The *Confession* was banned in Russia but, like many of Tolstoy's controversial works, it circulated unofficially and was eventually published abroad. As his crisis subsided, Tolstoy began a thorough investigation of the Orthodox Church and the Bible. Church tradition and even the Gospels, he decided, must somehow have distorted Christ's teachings: How was it possible to condone evils such as executions and wars after Christ had taught pity, forgiveness, and love? After much study, Tolstoy discovered a possible solution: emphasizing the notion of nonresistance to evil taken from Matthew. This one rule, he concluded, could put an end to violence and promote love. Reexamining the Scriptures, Tolstoy then derived from them five commandments that he thought expressed the essence of Christ's teaching: 1) avoid anger; 2) avoid lust; 3) never bind yourself by taking an oath; 4) do not resist evil; and 5) love even your enemies. By rejecting what he considered mystical elements in Christian doctrine, Tolstoy arrived at a closely reasoned answer to the question, "How should we live?" His religious study resulted in two banned works, *Kritika dogmaticheskogo bogosloviia* (*A Criticism of Dogmatic Theology*, 1880) and *Soedinenie i perevod chetyrekh evangelii* (*A Translation and Harmony of the Four Gospels*, 1881). Tolstoy now perplexed his family and friends as he persistently proclaimed his truths that would save the world.

In March of 1881 terrorists killed Tsar Alexander II and were condemned to death. Tolstoy, whose new-found faith obliged him to protest capital punishment, wrote to Alexander III quoting Matthew ("Love your enemies"), urging Christian forgiveness, and even stressing the joy that a pardon, as an act of royal goodness, would bring to the

Russian people. The tsar's response was reportedly that he could not pardon the murderers of his father, and the terrorists were hanged.

In September the Tolstoys moved to Moscow for the sake of their children's education; Sonya was delighted to return to a more cultured society. Her health was poor, however, and their eleventh child was born the next month. Tolstoy himself was horrified when he visited a Moscow slum area: in 1882 he published an appeal for aid to the poor, "O perepisi v Moskve" ("On the Moscow Census"), and began writing the social treatise "Tak chto zhe nam delat'?" ("What Then Must We Do?"). He and Sonya quarreled frequently, for she thought that he was neglecting his own family while trying to save the world. Much of the next year was devoted to *V chem moia vera, (What I Believe)*, a book that argues against seeking personal gain; it vividly delineates the author's own religious struggles and culminates in a moralistic plea to follow the teachings of Christ. By this time, the tsarist police were keeping Tolstoy under routine surveillance.

Late in 1883 Tolstoy met Vladimir Chertkov, a spiritual brother who—as an increasingly imperious disciple—was to become a major factor in promulgating Tolstoy's ideas and a disruptive force within his family. Then twenty-nine, Chertkov had resigned as captain of the Horse Guards to live on his estate, where he worked to improve the lives of the peasants. Tolstoy encouraged him to etablish Posrednik (The Intermediary), a publishing house that brought good literature within the financial reach of the masses. (During its first four years it sold twelve million booklets at one and a half kopecks each.[16]) Chertkov also worked to promote dissemination abroad of Tolstoy's censored works, some of which he himself translated into English.

During the summer of 1884, men and women from all walks of life began appearing at Yasnaya Polyana, disciples whom Sonya called "the dark people." Tolstoy himself now took up shoemaking and plunged into physical labor. He also became a vegetarian for life and gave up wine, hunting, and—though unsuccessfully at first—smoking. As Tolstoy and Chertkov developed and acknowledged their spiritual intimacy, Sonya suffered. The ardent disciple now had access to the master's most private thoughts, which frequently focused upon Sonya's inability to share his convictions. Tolstoy contributed stories to the Intermediary and came to depend heavily on Chertkov's promotional and financial abilities.

The rift between Tolstoy and his family widened as he continually attempted to convert them to his views. Sonya, who wanted no more children, was in a state bordering on hysteria prior to the birth of her twelfth child, Alexandra. She also objected to passages in Tolstoy's writing that she thought contained offensive references to the family. Moreover, she was working to bring out a new edition of his works, and argued bitterly with Chertkov, who wanted some of them for the Intermediary. She fought desperately for the funds needed to sustain the family's standard of living—a standard that, though a violation of Tolstoy's beliefs, she considered both proper and essential. In December of 1885, Tolstoy abandoned Moscow for the country, leaving Sonya a long letter in which he summed up their relationship as he saw it: "A struggle to the death is going on between us. Either God's works, or not God's works."[17]

In January of 1886 Sonya's four-year-old son Alyosha died of the croup. Added to her grief was Tolstoy's intimacy with Chertkov, with whom he now exchanged diaries. Still, she was pleased that her husband had returned to artistic literature, publishing "Smert' Ivana Il'icha" ("The Death of Ivan Ilych") in 1886 and *Vlast' t'my* (*The Power of Darkness*) in 1887. Late in 1887, Tolstoy tersely evaluated his twenty-five years of marriage in his diary: "could have been better."[18] In March of 1888 Sonya gave birth to Vanichka, her thirteenth child.

By this time Tolstoy had succeeded in alienating many friends, some of whom feared he was insane, and in alarming both the Orthodox Church and the tsarist government. The police watched as pilgrims from all over the world came to Yasnaya Polyana. Tolstoyan agricultural colonies were being established by disciples in other parts of the country. Tolstoy himself continued to follow his five commandments, living as simply and self-sufficiently as possible, even emptying his own chamber pot. In 1889, he finished *Kreitserova sonata* (*The Kreutzer Sonata*), a story whose unbalanced narrator advocates sexual abstinence even in marriage. Sonya sadly copied out the manuscript, accurately envisioning the furor it would cause. Tolstoy, who at sixty still felt intense sexual desire, feared that Sonya might become pregnant again, but she did not. The censor forbade publication of the work (unofficial copies circulated widely) until Sonya, through a personal interview with Alexander III, obtained permission to print it in Tolstoy's collected works in 1891.

How We Should Live, 1890–1910

Attempting to live in accordance with his beliefs, Tolstoy in 1891 officially renounced the rights to almost all his works published after

1881, although earlier works still benefited the family financially. He also soon gave away all his property (valued at 580,000 roubles) in ten shares, to Sonya and their nine living children.

When terrible famine swept much of European Russia in 1891–92, Tolstoy labored to set up relief centers despite his moral reluctance: he believed that organized charity merely perpetuated the evil of a society divided into rich and poor. In Moscow, Sonya wrote a moving appeal for desperately needed funds that was published in all the Russian newspapers and even translated abroad. Tolstoy himself published an article, "Strashnyi vopros" ("A Terrible Question"), that disturbed the authorities, who had been trying to suppress news of the disaster. Donations poured in from all over the world, and there were rumors that Tolstoy might be exiled or even imprisoned. Countess Alexandra Tolstaya used her influence, and he returned to Yasnaya Polyana in July of 1892. Despite much resistance (some local priests called him "Antichrist") Tolstoy had successfully brought relief to the peasants, feeding as many as 16,000 people daily. Even the proceeds from his recently staged play *Plody prosveshcheniia* (*The Fruits of Enlightenment*) went to this cause. During their heroic joint effort, the Tolstoys had enjoyed a relatively harmonious relationship.

In 1893 Tolstoy completed *Tsarstvo bozhie vnutri vas* (*The Kingdom of God is within You*), published the next year in Berlin. Denouncing both church and state for their oppression of the masses, this book-length essay urged moral enlightenment and advocated nonresistance to evil, just at a time when persecution of Tolstoyans was increasing. During the summer of 1894 Tolstoy's relationship with Sonya again deteriorated. Early the next year, quarrels and the death of their last-born child, Vanichka, from scarlet fever, brought Sonya close to both suicide and insanity. She then sought release in a passion for music that included the composer and pianist Sergey Tanaev. Sonya's obvious attraction to the plump, forty-year-old bachelor embarrassed her family: at fifty-two, this emotionally distraught woman was behaving like an infatuated schoolgirl. Tolstoy at first treated Tanaev with exaggerated politeness, but in 1898 he appealed to Sonya in writing, threatening to go abroad and begging her to break off relations with Tanaev. But she continued to pursue the musician, who finally turned away from her in 1904. There is no evidence that they were ever more than friends.

In March of 1895, Tolstoy published "Khoziain i rabotnik" ("Master and Man"), the story of a merchant who abandons his servant in a snowstorm but returns and dies saving the man's life with the warmth of his own body. During the summer, the authorities brutally punished several communities of Dukhobors, a peasant sect with beliefs similar to Tolstoy's, for refusing to serve in the army, and Tolstoy's own followers who resisted military service were also persecuted. The next year Tolstoy suggested to the authorities that they take measures against him instead, but they chose to deny him martyrdom. Early in 1897 Chertkov and two other prominent Tolstoyans who supported the Dukhobors were exiled for five years. When the Dukhobors were finally permitted to emigrate to Canada, Tolstoy raised funds, including a large advance for his third and last major novel, *Voskresenie (Resurrection)*. He later wrote an article on the evils of patriotism, which he considered an immoral feeling that leads to violence.

In 1897 Tolstoy finished *Chto takoe iskusstvo? (What Is Art?)*, a statement he had been formulating for the past fifteen years. This highly controversial essay condemns most of its author's own literary creations, as well as many other classics including Shakespeare's *Hamlet* and Beethoven's Ninth Symphony. Attacking much established art as elitist and corrupting, Tolstoy declared that true art must readily reach the masses and sincerely promote the brotherhood of man. Among those he praised in the essay was Charles Dickens, whom Tolstoy termed (in 1904) "the greatest novel writer of the 19th century."[19] Heavily censored, *What Is Art?* was published in 1898 and panned by most critics.

Tolstoy finished *Resurrection* in December of 1899; it appeared serially to an enthusiastic reception. Despite substantial alteration by the censor, the published novel still ridiculed both the Church and its leading official, Konstantin Pobedonostsev. Early in 1901 Pobedonostsev drew up an edict excommunicating Tolstoy from the Orthodox Church: it charged him with a list of specific heresies and urged him to repent. After the document, signed by several leading ecclesiastics, was published, letters of sympathy and condemnation (mostly the former) poured in from all over the world. Tolstoy himself first reacted with "Tsariu i ego pomoshchnikam" ("An Appeal to the Tsar and His Officials"), a plea for human rights and religious freedom that was largely ignored. He then published a heavily censored "Otvet na opredelenie Sinoda" ("Reply to the Holy Synod's Edict"), explaining that many of the charges against him were false but adding that he could not change his present faith.

Tolstoy soon returned to Yasnaya Polyana, where a long struggle over his will began: Sonya was outraged by his intention not to allow the family to receive more of the proceeds from his works. During the summer Tolstoy was struck by malaria, and traveled to the Crimea. A few years before he had displayed astonishing physical strength and endurance, but now, at seventy-three, he was besieged by numerous afflictions, including typhoid fever. While in the Crimea, Tolstoy was visited by Maxim Gorky, whose writing he had criticized but admired, and by Anton Chekhov, whose stories he had praised highly but whose plays he thought "even worse" than Shakespeare's.

Despite his maladies, Tolstoy continued to write, and early in 1902 finished the long essay, "Chto takoe religiia i v chem sushchnost' ee?" ("What Is Religion?"). He also sent a letter beginning "Dear Brother" to Nicholas II. Urging social reforms upon the tsar, he warned that cruel oppression by both church and state had brought the people to the brink of rebellion. Tolstoy thus predicted the revolution of 1905. In "Obrashchenie k dukhovenstvu" ("An Appeal to the Clergy") he likened the teachings of the Church to an inoculation rendering people immune to true Christianity. Tolstoy protested the Jewish pogroms in Kishinyov in 1903 and wrote three tales to be published for the victims' financial benefit. In 1904 he finished *Hadji Murat,* a short novel of brutality and bravery in the Caucasus, as well as his controversial "O Shekspire i o drame" ("Shakespeare and the Drama"). Applying the criteria of *What Is Art?,* this essay attempts to destroy the reputations of *King Lear* and Shakespeare's other plays. When the Russo-Japanese War began, Tolstoy wrote an essay (published in England by Chertkov) deploring what he saw as futile slaughter. After the revolution of 1905, he condemned efforts to establish a constitutional government since he now viewed all governments as evil. His condemnation of violence had become no less extreme: asked if killing by a revolutionary was not superior to killing by a policeman, he likened the two to "cat-shit and dog-shit," both of which have unpleasant odors.[20]

When Chertkov was finally permitted to return to Yasnaya Polyana in 1905, Sonya's anxieties about publication rights intensified. In September of 1906, she barely survived an operation for a tumor of the womb, and Tolstoy searched for signs of spiritual regeneration within her. As the newly established legislature faltered during the years 1906–7, Tolstoy became more convinced that Russia was wrong to imitate Western civilization. In an article called "O znachenii russkoi revoliutsii" ("The Significance of the Russian Revolution"), he viewed the Russian people as "Eastern," and saw their salvation in agriculture (as opposed to industry) and in the ideal of nonresistance to evil. "Why not suppose," he wrote, "that people will rejoice in and compete not for riches or luxury, but for simplicity, moderation, and kindness to one another?"[21] He also wrote to the prime minister, Peter Stolypin, strongly urging him to read Henry George and to consider abolishing private ownership of property.

Tolstoy began suffering fainting spells early in 1908, but he continued to work, relying increasingly on a dictaphone sent to him by Thomas Edison. When twelve peasants were hanged for armed intrusion on a landowner's estate he wrote "Ne mogu molchat'" ("I Cannot Be Silent"), an article in which he denied that such killings could promote the general welfare. He even expressed a desire to be hanged himself, so that the executions would not promote his welfare at least. The article caused a great uproar. An official celebration planned for Tolstoy's eightieth birthday was cancelled because of opposition from the Church and the government, but thousands of people, including many of the world's leading figures, sent their congratulations. That summer, Chertkov settled on a nearby estate and took a proprietary attitude toward Tolstoy's life, thoughts, and works. Sonya objected strenuously, and bitter quarrels ensued, many of them dutifully recorded by Chertkov.

In 1909, police persecution of Tolstoy's friends intensified, and Chertkov was forced to move away. In September, Tolstoy received a letter from Gandhi expressing admiration for various of his works including *The Kingdom of God Is Within You*. (After Tolstoy's death, Gandhi referred to him as "the highest moral authority."[22]) Meanwhile, Sonya was becoming increasingly hysterical on the subject of publication rights. In November, Tolstoy signed a will (kept secret from Sonya) leaving control of his works to his daughter Alexandra, who, with Chertkov's aid, was to make his writings public property. In June of 1910, Tolstoy visited Chertkov. After an ugly struggle between Sonya and Chertkov over control of his diaries, Tolstoy placed them in a bank vault. His relationship with Sonya became intolerable. She accused him of homosexual relations with Chertkov, constantly spied upon him, and even pretended that she had poisoned herself. Tolstoy thought of escape more and more often.

Incited by a renewed offer of one million roubles for publication rights, Sonya badgered her husband and searched relentlessly for his latest will. On 28 October Tolstoy awoke at three A.M. to hear her going through papers in his study. Filled with indignation, he wrote her a letter in which he thanked Sonya for forty-eight years of married life, urged mutual forgiveness, and asked her not to try to follow him. He then woke his doctor and his daughter Alexandra, who helped him to pack. Leaving his wife asleep, Tolstoy rode with his doctor in surreptitious haste to the railroad station where he took the train. Illness forced Tolstoy off the train at Astapovo, where he was given the stationmaster's house. Ironically, his attempt to find peace and solitude now became the focus of intense international interest. The station swarmed with journalists, who dispatched hourly bulletins on Tolstoy's condition. Sonya arrived in a private train but was permitted to see her husband only when he was apparently too ill to recognize her. Attended by his doctor and children (Alexandra, Tanya and Sergey), Tolstoy died on 7 November. His body was buried at Yasnaya Polyana, as he had requested, at the very spot where—according to his brother Nikolay—there was hidden a little green stick inscribed with the secret for bringing happiness and love to everyone.

Chapter Two
Childhood, Boyhood, and Youth

Tolstoy was barely twenty-four when *Childhood* appeared in 1852 and established him overnight as a major writer of his time. To be sure, Nekrasov, editor of the *Contemporary*, had changed its title to *A History of My Childhood*, which dismayed Tolstoy since he had worked through several drafts to lift particular biographical and autobiographical elements to a representative and universally valid level. "Who is interested in the history of *my* childhood?"[1] he wrote angrily to Nekrasov. The title, he declared, contradicted the idea of the work.

Tolstoy had planned to write a novel entitled *Four Periods of Growth*. The fourth part, never written, was to deal with the happier, more positive second half of youth. In the trilogy *Childhood, Boyhood, and Youth*, the generally autobiographical Nicholas Irtenyev tells his own story as he reminisces "decades later" (1:311). What emerges is a mixture of portraits, scenes, episodes, digressive reflection, and psychological analysis. The narrator examines his own developing consciousness, attempting to relate a microscopic analysis of individual moments to large patterns of meaning. Each approach enhances the other, though sometimes less successfully than in Tolstoy's more mature works.

While working on *Childhood*, Tolstoy penned a message entitled "To my Readers," in which he anticipated objections to it. He had tried to write, he explained, from the heart rather than from the head. "But when you write from the heart, there are so many thoughts in your head, so many images in your imagination, so many memories in your heart, that their expression is incomplete, inadequate, halting and crude."[2] He asked his reader to be "sensitive" and "understanding," to find a response in his soul for "every sound in my own soul."

The first reviews of *Childhood* were highly favorable, though critics reproached the author for "the excessiveness of his analysis and the minuteness of his descriptions."[3] Konstantin Aksakov, for example, somewhat captiously contended: "Count Tolstoy's analysis often notices trivia, not worthy of attention, which pass across the soul like a small cloud, leaving no trace; once noticed and analyzed they take on a meaning greater than they really have and hence become unreal."[4] Late in life Tolstoy himself characteristically disparaged the work, finding it poorly written, muddled, and insincere. He had been too dependent, he decided, on Rodolphe Töpffer and Laurence Sterne. Actually Dickens and Rousseau (both of whom he greatly admired) may have been even more important influences on it. There are several striking parallels between *David Copperfield* and Tolstoy's trilogy, as R. F. Christian has shown; the affinity with Rousseau, he observes, is most clearly seen in "the *penchant* for self-analysis and the urge to confess."[5]

Aspiration

As ten-year-old Nicholas Irtenyev matures, he makes increasingly complex Tolstoyan efforts toward self-improvement. At first his aspirations seem spontaneous; later they give way to posing and painful self-consciousness. However, a relentless, searching honesty unifies the trilogy.

Early in *Childhood*, Nicholas and his brother Volodya run upstairs, "squealing and tramping," to prepare for the hunt (1:29). While dressing, they try to look as much as possible like huntsmen: "One of the main methods of accomplishing this was to stuff our trousers into our boots," he recalls. This perspective of gentle humor is reflected in the work's very language, which, like the two boys, faintly strains at self-importance. The same technique communicates Nicholas's feeling of grand excitement as he mounts his horse and makes "various evolutions" around the yard. A hunter then warns him not to run over the dogs: "'Don't worry; this is not my first time,' I answered proudly." But as the boy soon sadly realizes by watching his own shadow, he was far from presenting the "fine appearance" to which he so earnestly aspired (1:30).

That evening little Nicholas decides to draw a picture of the hunt even though he has only blue paint.

Having very energetically sketched a blue boy riding a blue horse and some blue dogs, I didn't know for sure if it was all right to draw a blue hare, and I ran to Papa's study to confer with him about it. Papa was reading something, and to my question "Are there any blue hares?" he answered, without raising his head: "Yes, my boy, there are." Returning to the round table, I sketched a blue hare, then found it necessary to turn the blue hare into a bush. I didn't like the bush either; I made it into a tree, the tree—into a haystack, the haystack—into a cloud, and, finally, I smeared up the whole paper so much with blue paint that I tore it up with vexation and went off to doze in the high-backed armchair. (1:39–40)

As before, Nicholas's gently humorous self-importance is reflected in the language itself ("to confer with him," "found it necessary"). Also similarly, the boy's intentions are depicted with a warm, unabashed honesty. There is a natural purity about the episode which makes it surprisingly unimportant whether Nicholas finally "succeeded" in drawing his blue hare. The description generates a self-contained reality in which the boy's blunders almost magically redeem themselves as each apparent failure gives rise to a new inspiration. In this atmosphere of persistently hopeful aspiration, even Nicholas's final repose in the armchair acquires a touch of triumph.

For his grandmother's name-day celebration, Nicholas aspires to write a poem and to make a handsome appearance. For a long time he tries to smooth down the tufts of hair on his abundantly pomaded head. But whenever he stops to "test their obedience," the tufts "would rise up and stick out on all sides, giving my face a most ridiculous expression," (1:57). When it is time to present his poem, Nicholas blushes, and "large drops of sweat" appear on his nose and forehead: "My ears burned, I felt my entire body shake and perspire, and I shifted from one foot to the other without moving forward." Nicholas is mortified as his grandmother then reads his poem with, it seems to him, "a mocking smile." In his painful confusion, he decides that the phrase "like our own dear mother" (in his poem) "clearly proves" that he had never loved his own mother, now dead, and has forgotten her (1:59).

In *Boyhood,* Nicholas grandly imagines himself helping two house serfs in the future. "Petrovskoe [an estate] will belong to me, and Vasily and Masha will be my serfs," he thinks. "I'll say, 'Send Masha to me.' . . . I'll say, 'Vasily . . . Here are a thousand roubles for you. Marry her and may God give you happiness,' and I myself will go off into the sitting room" (1:165). This magnanimous, self-dramatizing episode resembles several others in Tolstoy's early works. In *Utro po-meshchika* (*A Landowner's Morning*), for example, the Tolstoyan hero Nekhlyudov makes several attempts to help his serfs, but he is partially blinded by his aim of deriving pleasure from his efforts.

After planning to help the serfs, Nicholas devotes an entire year to what he terms "a solitary moral life, concentrated in my own self." He struggles with various abstract questions, attempting to apply to his own life the "great and useful truths" which, he imagines, he is *"the first"* to discover. These include the rather masochistic theory that a person accustomed to suffering cannot be unhappy. Young Nicholas therefore undergoes painful physical exercises of endurance and self-flagellation. In addition, he attains "the verge of insanity" by his mental exertions. Solipcistically imagining that "nothing and no one existed in the entire world besides myself," the boy enters a vicious circle of thinking about his own thought. "However," he writes, "the philosophical discoveries I made exceedingly flattered my self-esteem: I often imagined myself a great man, discovering new truths for the good of all mankind, and I looked upon other mortals with a proud awareness of my own merit. . . " (1:168). This Tolstoyan aspiration is then typically qualified by the honest admission that Nicholas could not display his feeling of great worth, and even felt painfully self-conscious in the presence of others.

Early in *Youth,* Nicholas resolves to formulate for himself "a schedule of duties and occupations"—the rules he will follow "unwaveringly" his entire life. Having prepared a notebook headed "Rules of Life," however, he stares at it quite helplessly for a long time. A servant then announces that the priest has come to read the precepts of the Church, creating a rather humorous irony: the same Russian word (*pravila*) is used for the "precepts" as for the "rules" of life whose potential creation they interrupt (1:200). Hiding his still empty notebook, Nicholas looks in the mirror and brushes his hair "upwards, which, I was convinced, gave me a pensive expression," and goes down to the sitting room.

Nicholas's intense concern with his own physical appearance can be related to Tolstoy's use of "body language." Characteristic examples occur early in *Childhood,* as Nicholas observes the steward Yakov: "I noticed from the quickness with which his fingers moved that he wanted to object" (1:19), or: "From the expression of Yakov's face and his fingers it was evident that the last order gave him great pleasure" (1:21). Tolstoy greatly favored such eloquent physical descriptions.[6] A contemporary critic, while praising *Youth* highly, wrote to Tolstoy as follows: "You are sometimes on the point of saying that so-and-so's thigh indicated that he wished to travel to India!"[7]

While trying to compose his "Rules of Life," Nicholas wonders: "Why is everything so beautiful and clear in my heart but comes out so ugly on paper and in life generally, when I wish to put some of my ideas into practice?" He himself soon provides a fascinating perspective on the matter: "How harmful it is to think, and still more harmful to

say, much that seems very noble but which should forever be hidden
from others in the heart of each person . . . noble words seldom go
with noble deeds. I am convinced that the very fact of declaring a good
intention makes it difficult—and even for the most part impossible—
to carry out that good intention." (1:249) This is a characteristic Tolstoyan formulation. Tolstoy's own diaries are filled with good resolu-
tions, and admissions that they were soon broken. Apparently, the very
articulation of a firm resolve to reform rendered action less necessary,
perhaps even unlikely. A relieved conscience, he evidently found, can
lead to dangerous overconfidence.

Four pages after setting out his theory on the harm of uttering good
intentions, Nicholas confides to his friend Dmitry that he is "definitely
(*reshitel'no*) in love with" Sonya. Despite Dmitry's "indifference," Nicholas then tells him all about his love and his plans for a happily
married future: "And, strangely enough, no sooner did I relate in detail
the entire force of my feelings, than at that very instant I felt these
feelings begin to diminish." The word *reshitel'no* also means "resolute-
ly." Nicholas is thus on the verge of trying to convince himself of his
own noble feelings, and of protesting too much. The fact that Nicholas
ignores his friend's "indifference" to his outpourings points up the increasingly self-centered quality of his aspirations.

When Nicholas at last succeeds in formulating some "rules" to follow, they are both superficial and self-centered. The goal he finally sets
is to be comme il faut. "For me, *comme il faut* was not only an important
merit, an excellent quality, a perfection that I wished to attain; it was
an essential condition of life without which there could be neither happiness, nor fame, nor anything good in the world (1:286)." This fab-
ulous quality, we are told, had several components. First and foremost
one must have an excellent command of French, especially pronuncia-
tion; second, "fingernails—long, manicured, and clean." Third, one
should be skillful in bowing, dancing, and conversing. "Fourth, and
very important, was an indifference to everything and a perpetual
expression of elegant, scornful boredom." Nicholas now finds it "horrible to recall" how much valuable time he wasted, at sixteen, on efforts to achieve this state of being. He now sees as "especially evil" his
former conviction that a *comme il faut* person "was already fulfilling his
purpose [in life] and was even becoming superior to most others."

Not surprisingly, Nicholas's egotistical concern with superficial
qualities isolates him. His attitude combines a blind snobbishness with
the painfully paralyzing assumption that others can read his mind. In

short, he succeeds in spinning about himself a cocoon of self-consciousness which falls away only under the blow of failure in his examinations, after which he resolves to renew his striving for self-perfection.

Injustice

As *Childhood* opens, a dead fly, killed by the boys' tutor Karl Ivanych, lands upon young Nicholas's head. The boy awakens keenly offended: Why does the tutor not kill flies around his older brother's bed? Almost at once, however, Nicholas shamefully realizes that Karl Ivanych is in fact a kindly man. Not long after this, the maid Natalya Savishna scolds Nicholas for soiling a table cloth, but then displays such gentle kindness that the boy's angry sobs yield to tears of love and shame. It is emphasized later that both Karl Ivanych and Natalya Savishna had been victims of injustice in the past; though they suspect their faithfulness is not fully appreciated, they now devotedly serve the Irtenyevs. Karl Ivanych's life story, which takes up three successive chapters of *Boyhood,* could seem disproportionately long except that it helps to focus Nicholas's developing awareness of cruelty and injustice.

Late in his life, Tolstoy singled out the story of Joseph from the Bible as having made an "enormous" impression on him before the age of fourteen.[8] In Karl Ivanych's life story, which greatly impresses young Nicholas, Karl's rejection of amorous advances from his trusting master's wife parallels Joseph's reaction in a similar situation: as Karl Ivanych explains, he refused to repay his master's goodness with "ingratitude" (1:139). The motif of ingratitude points up Nicholas's developing awareness of injustice. When Karl Ivanych, who is no longer needed by the family, learns of his dismissal, he gives the boy a dictation stating that the most cruel of all passions is "Ingratitude" (1:24); Natalya Savishna's request for permission to marry another servant had been interpreted as "ingratitude" (1:45), and she was strictly punished. Soviet criticism of Tolstoy's trilogy has predictably emphasized his "unmasking" of the false morality of gentry society.[9] It would be more to the point to note that young Nicholas's concern about various forms of injustice reflects a developing Tolstoyan emphasis upon the problem of how we should live.

In *Childhood,* little Nicholas listens uneasily to Countess Kornakova's opinion that it is necessary and beneficial to "beat" one's children (1:61). He later meets her smug, "beefy" son Étienne, fifteen, and decides that he "was exactly the way a boy who is flogged would be"

(1:75). Nicholas then learns that Etienne would always sit on the coachman's box and use the whip: he greatly enjoyed "giving it to those who passed by." Clearly, the inference is that Étienne has been brought up to pass on brutality to others; the boy routinely makes the servants pay for his own mistakes.

In between the descriptions of Countess Kornakova and her son, Nicholas describes his passionate affection for a handsome young play-mate, Seryozha Ivin. The countess's theory of "beating" and its ugly results thus frame what seems at first to be a pleasant contrast. Nicholas, we are told, developed an "irresistible attraction" to Seryozha, whose stoic heroism greatly impressed him. He also feared displeasing him. They all sometimes played with Ilinka Grap, a thin, pale lad "with a birdlike little face and a good-natured, submissive expression" (1:67–71). One day Seryozha bullied the frail Ilinka cruelly, and Nicholas joined in. "I am quite unable to explain the cruelty of what I did. How was it that I did not approach him, did not defend or console him?" Is it possible, Nicholas now wonders, that love for Seryozha and the desire to win his approval stifled all compassion for Ilinka? Then how despicable, he concludes, were that love and that desire, "the only dark spots on the pages of my childhood recollections." Nicholas's cru-elty thus seems to derive from an effort to emulate Seryozha. His ret-rospective shame is aggravated by the very intensity of his former admiration. As a painful but essential influence upon Nicholas's moral growth, Seryozha is built up and then pointedly undermined.

Also in *Childhood,* Nicholas experiences "something like first love" (1:36) for Katya, the daughter of his sister's music teacher. Early in *Boyhood,* he observes that Katya has become "strange" (1:122), rather serious and sad. She denies being "strange," but explains that they must eventually separate because "you are rich . . . and we are poor." Nicholas is shocked, painfully ashamed of being rich: "Have you ever suddenly noticed, reader, . . . that your view of things has completely changed, as if everything you had seen before had suddenly turned another, as yet unknown side to you? A moral change of that kind took place in me . . . which I regard as the beginning of my boyhood" (1:123).

Nicholas's relationship with Katya has now been undermined. Just as the coerciveness of Seryozha's attitude left dark spots on Nicholas's childhood, the tyranny of social convention now "darkens" his rela-tionship with Katya. Unlike Seryozha, however, Katya is quite inno-cent, and thus the injustice here seems more complex. Another difference is that instead of reevaluating his attitude in retrospect, Nicholas now does so immediately, in a sign of the increased maturity of boyhood. His aside to the reader about a sudden change in one's view of things is a useful description of "making strange," one of Tolstoy's favorite literary devices.[10] When a character abruptly sees something in a new light (or for the first time), the reader tends to share more vividly in the experience. A good example can be found late in *Youth,* when Nicholas returns to the country house in which he had lived as a child: "Everything was the same, only it had all grown smaller and lower, while I seemed to have grown taller, heavier, and coarser. . ." (1:275).

At the end of *Boyhood,* Nicholas develops an intimate friendship with Dmitry Nekhlyudov; they agree to "confess everything" to each other. As *Youth* begins, this friendship opens up for Nicholas a new view of life: "man's purpose is to strive for moral perfection" (1:189). The decision to apply this idea to his own life he now considers "the beginning of my youth." As in his pivotal relationships with Seryozha and Kataya, Nicholas's friendship with Dmitry eventually exposes him to a form of injustice. They quarrel bitterly, and he concludes that their intimate confessions have become "weapons" that they now use unfairly against each other (1:322). Still, Nicholas retains the resolve to strive for moral perfection that began his youth. As with Seryozha and Katya, his intimacy with Dmitry thus provided a temporary but indispensable impetus to his moral development. The painful but positive moral growth resulting from disillusionment was to become a crucial element of *War and Peace.*

Death

R. F. Christian has suggested that the focal point of *Childhood* is not so much the hero but a "pattern" retrospectively imposed on his life by the narrator: behind the happiness of childhood lurks the inescapable and incomprehensible reality of death.[11] This pattern, he finds, culminates in the carefully juxtaposed deaths of Natalya Savishna and Nicholas's mother.

Before she dies, Nicholas's mother writes in a letter to her husband: "I shall no longer be with you, but I am firmly convinced that my love will never leave you, and this thought is so comforting to my heart that I calmly and fearlessly await the approach of death" (1:91). However, she then declares uncertainty: "I am calm, . . . but why are these tears choking me?" Moreover, she has written these sections of the letter in French, a language which the nobility in Tolstoy's works frequently use to express artificial or superficial attitudes. We are thus not entirely surprised to learn that despite her calm fearlessness, Nicholas's mother died "in terrible agony" (1:95).

Natalya Savishna's death, which soon follows and ends *Childhood,* provides a sharp contrast with this. The simple peasant woman leaves her affairs in perfect order, even providing money for the poor. She then dies with God's name and "a joyous smile" upon her lips (1:106). Natalya could die without fear, we learn, because of her unshakeable religious faith: "Her entire life had been pure, disinterested love and self-abnegation." The natural woman's radiant smile contrasts didactically with the society lady's agony. And this is but one of three similar interrelated contrasts.

Prior to her death, Natalya Savishna had suffered for two months from her illness, bearing her sufferings with true Christian patience. The prelude to her death is a long and painful one (eased somewhat by her faith) as opposed to the calmness of Nicholas's mother (slightly undermined by her tears). Their respectively joyous and agonized deaths are thus abrupt reversals of what we expect, though nevertheless faintly anticipated.

The third contrast turns on the reactions of Natalya Savishna and Nicholas's grandmother to the death of his mother. His grandmother's grief is helpless, ostentatious and rebellious; Natalya adopts an attitude of practical, sensible resignation. Nicholas recollects that he sympathized more with Natalya's sadness, although he does not know why (1:104). Tolstoy would later suggest throughout *War and Peace* that people who resist the current of fate experience defeat—whereas those who flow with the tide ultimately emerge victorious. Here Nicholas instinctively prefers the natural, resigned reaction to the self-dramatized, rebellious one. But there is perhaps a still more significant factor. Whereas Natalya Savishna comforts little Nicholas and helps him accept his mother's death as constructively as possible, his grandmother withdraws into herself; in her hysteria she even fails, temporarily, to recognize the child. In both *War and Peace* and *Anna Karenina,* Tolstoy later depicted the ability to help others spontaneously and selflessly in times of crisis as a supremely admirable trait.

The developing attitude of young Nicholas himself toward death is also an important theme in the trilogy. In the chapter following the description of his mother's death (entitled "Grief") the boy gazes for a long time at her body and lapses into a strange state of oblivion: "I lost consciousness of my existence and experienced some kind of exalted, ineffably pleasing and sad delight" (1:96). In restrospect, he believes that "only this one minute of self-forgetfulness was genuine grief." Although he wept frequently, Nicholas explains, his sadness was "insincere and unnatural" because he was trying to impress other people. Since this passage precedes the descriptions of his grandmother's and Natalya Savishna's reactions, it helps to explain Nicholas's preference for the latter.

At his mother's funeral, Nicholas sees the frightened face of a five-year-old girl who stares wide-eyed at the corpse and screams in a frenzied voice. He himself then screams "in a voice which, I think, was even more terrible than the one that had struck me" and runs out of the room (1:99). Not only do we experience the terror of the tiny girl, exposed to death at such an early age; we also share young Nicholas's horrified reaction to her terror. Tolstoy would use this doubly vivid form of "making strange" to evoke the horrors of war in his *Sevastopol Stories*.

Nicholas is inspired by Natalya Savishna, with her unshakeable religious faith, as he puts it in a one-sentence paragraph: "She accomplished the best and greatest deed in this life: she died without regret or fear" (1:107). The word "best" may seem slightly ironic in this context, but it is used quite characteristically. In *War and Peace*, periods of heightened consciousness, no matter how disillusioning or painful, are termed "best moments" if they lead to positive personal growth.

Near the end of *Boyhood*, when Nicholas's grandmother dies, he feels neither admiration nor pity. Instead he experiences "an oppressive fear of death—that is, the dead body vividly and unpleasantly reminds me that I too must die some day, a feeling which for some reason most people confuse with grief" (1:176). Earlier, in a passage that resists translation into English, Nicholas had observed the impact of his mother's death upon his grandmother:

she was looking straight at me, but apparently she did not see me. Her lips slowly began to smile, and she started to speak in a touching, tender voice: "Come here, my dear, come over here, my angel." I thought she was addressing me, and I walked up closer, but she was not looking at me. "Oh, if you only knew, my dearest, how I have suffered and how glad I am now that you have come." I understood that she imagined seeing my mother, and I stopped. "And they told me that you were no more," she continued, frowning. "What nonsense! How could you die before me?" And she broke into horrible, hysterical laughter. (1:104)

The untranslatable effect here begins with the word "knew." In Russian the form *znala* makes it instantly clear that the boy's grandmother is addressing a female when she says "Oh, if you only knew." The words "glad that you have come" (*rada, chto ty priekhala*) sustain the faintly eerie impact of mistaken gender and, in addition, suggest that a very dear friend has come from far away. Tolstoy was later to employ a more subtle but strikingly similar technique in *War and Peace,* when the Countess Rostova learns that her son Petya has been killed.

During the third night the countess became very quiet for several minutes, and Natasha, in her chair, closed her eyes and propped up her head. The bed creaked. Natasha opened her eyes. The countess was sitting up in bed and speaking softly.
    "How glad I am that you have come. You're tired. Would you like some tea?" Natasha went up to her. "You've grown better looking and more manly," continued the countess, taking her daughter's hand.
    "Mama! What are you saying?"
    "Natasha, he is no more, no more!" And, embracing her daughter, the countess began to weep for the first time. (7:188)

In *Childhood,* the grandmother repeatedly seemed not to see Nicholas, thus providing clues to the mistake that results from her half-insane grief. Here, some English readers will realize the truth only when they encounter the word "manly." In Tolstoy's Russian, however, the countess's very first words have a deeply moving effect upon the reader. As in *Childhood,* the words "glad that you have come" (*rada, chto ty priekhal*) vividly and poignantly mistake the gender of the person ostensibly addressed, and also suggest that the dear apparition has come from far away. As in *Childhood,* these simple words suggest the touching truth that the speaker's great "gladness" derives from her anguished self-delusion.

Destiny

Tolstoy's concern with the workings of fate can be traced back to the beginning of *Childhood* and the dream that Nicholas invents merely to excuse his own tears, which anticipates his mother's early death. He thus becomes the first in a series of what can be called "unlikely prophets" in Tolstoy's works.[12] If such characters are mentally or physically deficient, their unexpected predictions tend to be still more ironic. Nicholas's mother believes that the "holy fool" Grisha's mutterings may well be prophetic; the peasant Kiryusha, she declares, "foretold the exact day and hour of death for deceased papa" (1:28).

The Russian academic custom of assigning examination questions by lot affords Tolstoy an opportunity to explore the workings of fate further. In *Youth* Nicholas draws, to his horror, the one mathematics question he has failed to prepare. But then a fellow student, Ikonin, who has just refused to trade questions, changes his mind at the last second, giving Nicholas the very question he had just finished preparing. This rather stylized episode leaves the reader wondering why Ikonin abruptly acted as he did and whether Nicholas, who had just struggled in vain to prepare the question he in fact drew, was somehow fated not to have to answer it. A somewhat similar last-second switch (in drawing lots) in Tolstoy's *Sevastopol Stories* results in death.

Also in *Youth,* Nicholas helps a workman to remove a winter window: "'If the frame comes out right away now, when I pull with him,' I thought, 'then it would be a sin to study any more today'" (1:191). Soon after the frame gives way, Nicholas sits on the sill and turns pensive. He then has a rapturously inspiring experience: spring itself seems to tell him through the open window that beauty, happiness, and virtue are one, a unity he can easily attain. "How could I not have understood this?" he wonders. "How bad I have formerly been; how good and happy I can be in the future!" What began as a rather playful testing of fate becomes an almost spiritual inspiration. Attempting to convey his experience to the reader, Nicholas describes the joy of life that one can feel through an open window on a blissful summer evening. As early as 1850 Tolstoy had wanted to write a story consisting of various scenes described "from the window,"[13] and his interest in this perspective has been traced to Rodolphe Töpffer.[14]

Perhaps the most striking series of fateful episodes in Tolstoy's works features a character gazing up at a lofty sky and experiencing what seems to be a crucial moment in his life. In chapter 32 of *Youth* (it bears the same title) Nicholas describes how he used to look outside at night and everything would take on a strange new aspect of beauty and happiness. *She* would then appear—the sad, voluptuous girl of his dreams for whom he would sacrifice even his life. And it seemed to him that "mysterious, majestic nature" and the bright, round, alluring moon, "which had stopped for some reason at one vague, lofty point

in the pale-blue sky, and yet which was everywhere and seemed to fill
the boundless entirety of space, and I, an insignificant worm, already
defiled by all the petty, meager human passions but endowed with all
the boundless mighty power of imagination and love—it seemed to me
at such moments that nature, the moon, and I were all one and the
same" (1:292). Such passages in Tolstoy's works typically suggest or
describe a transition to new attitudes and values. The observer (most
often, an autobiographical figure) seems to become attuned with a pivotal moment in his destiny. His focus usually moves upwards to the
moon, sun, or clouds, loftily suspended in the vastness of space, and
then returns to earth, where he himself is likened to a speck, an insect,
an atom, a worm. The reversion is humbling, yet inspirational. The
observer's very ability to apprehend the boundlessness of space seems
to enable his specklike existence to merge harmoniously, even pur-
posefully, with the vault overhead. As George Steiner has suggested of
three such passages in *War and Peace,* "the eye has returned inward to
find that the vast, exterior spaces have entered into the soul."[15]

Chapter Three
How Should We Live?

During 1853–63, the decade separating *Childhood* from *War and Peace,* Tolstoy published more than a dozen stories and short novels in addition to *Boyhood* and *Youth.* These works were partly inspired by his own experiences as a young landowner and a military man. The more important ones typically investigate various aspects of the question, How should we live? Also typically, the exploration of various possible answers tends to result in disenchantment.

Helping Others

Tolstoy's plan of 1852 to write a novel about a Russian landowner resulted in a twenty-chapter fragment, published in 1856, *Utro pomeshchika* (*A Landowner's Morning*). This autobiographical work records the frustrated attempts of Prince Nekhlyudov (aged nineteen, as was Tolstoy when he inherited Yasnaya Polyana) to help the serfs living on his lands. The well-meaning but naive prince visits three peasants and finds them exasperatingly resigned to their dire situation. The hero's efforts thus seem unpleasantly futile, as Turgenev was quick to point out, although Ernest Simmons maintains that "the real moral of the work" is that "so long as serfdom exists the master will be unable to better the lot of his peasants, despite the most disinterested endeavor to do so."[1]

While this is quite true, the prince's good intentions are not entirely disinterested: he seems somewhat self-centered, even egotistical. The work contains a persistent suggestion that pride poisons generosity. The prince's aunt (to whom he writes—in French—of his "holy and direct duty" as the story opens) quite bluntly accuses him of "excessive pride," then adds: "I believe in your sincerity when you say that you have no ambition, but you are deceiving yourself" (2:324).

Almost at once we encounter signs that the aunt is correct. The prince first visits a peasant who has requested some wooden plows. Learning that he intends to use them to prop up a dilapidated shed, the prince patiently reproaches his serf for not requesting the proper building materials, "evidently showing off his knowledge of the situation" (2:327). He also makes eloquent promises to help, "not knowing that such outpourings are incapable of awakening trust in any person, especially a Russian, who likes deeds, not words" (2:332). But the prince, we are told, "was so happy with the feeling he experienced that he couldn't help but pour it out." After Nekhlyudov's eloquence subsides, it develops that the peasant has no manure to fertilize his fields: he has sold the cow because his unfertilized fields cannot produce sufficient hay to feed it. "It's a strange vicious circle," the prince thinks, but Tolstoy emphasizes his awkward isolation by inserting "cercle vicieux" in the Russian text. Then, when the prince blushingly provides the money to buy a cow, the peasant thanks him for his "charity" with a "slightly sarcastic smile" (2:336).

After Prince Nekhlyudov struggles rather unsuccessfully with two additional "vicious circles," he wonders if his plans are "nonsense" (2:365). He then recalls experiencing, one May morning a year earlier, a moment of fateful inspiration. (The title of the story thus becomes aptly ambiguous.) Having dismissed thoughts of a "voluptuous woman" as "not it," the prince, lying on his back, had watched "the transparent morning clouds running above him across the deep, endless sky" and had rapturously resolved to improve the lot of his serfs: "I, who will do this for my own pleasure, I will delight in their gratitude, will see how I go farther and farther with each day towards my established goal." The prince's aim of altruism, it appears, was indeed self-serving, as his aunt had suspected. "Here I have been seeking happiness for a year now," he concludes, "and what have I found? . . . I am wasting the best years of my life" (2:367). Despite his disillusionment, the prince apparently fails to realize that one's primary purpose in helping others should not be one's own personal happiness. For him, at least, the Tolstoyan question of how we should live remains unanswered. The story ends with the prince musing rather enviously about the happy, healthy son of one of his more successful peasant families.

The provocative contrast between the prince's views and those of the simple, natural people he tries to help make it possible to view *A Landowner's Morning* as a protracted, rather didactic exercise in "making strange." Even the prince's little notebook in which he efficiently records his serf's requests and the chapter of "Maison Rustique" (an 1837 treatise on farm management) that he scans before setting out to visit them (2:325) appropriately introduce his unfamiliar perspective on their lives. The extensive contrasting of social and natural values in the story anticipates a much more complex one in *The Cossacks,* where the autobiographical hero, in a similar moment of Tolstoyan fateful inspiration, hits upon a less naive, but still flawed, theory of altruism.

In "Polikushka," a powerful novelette largely ignored by the critics when it was published in 1863, Tolstoy adopted a different approach to the problem of how to help others. Polikushka is a peasant with a bent for petty thievery and drunkenness. His owner, stressing her belief that he can reform, authorizes him to collect a large sum of money from a merchant in town. The weak but sensitive Polikushka repeatedly conquers the temptation to drink and hides the money in his cap with great care. In the very act of securing it, however, he tears his old cap and the money is lost. He then commits suicide, and in the ensuing commotion his wife leaves their baby son in his bath, where he drowns.

Polikushka's tragic efforts to justify the trust of his owner seem both more and less noble because he has so little choice in the matter. Her trust, however, seems only less admirable because she fails to appreciate its tyranny. As in *A Landowner's Morning,* serfdom creates a gap across which help cannot easily be given, whatever the motives of the giver.

Ivan Turgenev praised "Polikushka" but found the baby's death unnecessary.[2] In fact, however, the father's and son's deaths are carefully interrelated so that each reinforces the other. When Polikushka returns home without the money, we learn that "two subjects especially arrested his anxious, feverishly open eyes: the rope fastened to the cradle and the baby" (3:333). He unties the rope, his eyes "stopping" upon the child. This intense, repeated association of rope and baby is grimly prophetic. Polikushka leaves, and his wife bathes the baby, who is crying. A cry of terror then issues from the joiner's wife, who has found Polikushka hanging. Her report causes Polikushka's wife to release the baby, who slips, "pulling up his little legs," into the water. The joiner's wife describes the suicide: "I look, and his legs are swinging." Polikushka's wife then returns to find her baby drowned, "his little legs not moving" (3:335). This compressed series of interrelated details, however gruesome, renders the half-demented Polikushka's death considerably more vivid and touching. In a sense we are invited to ponder, he dies almost as helplessly as does his child.

Dying For Others

In 1853 and 1855 Tolstoy published two stories about military life in the Caucasus based upon his own first-hand experiences, "Nabeg"

(The Raid) and "Rubka lesa" (The Wood-felling). In these tales he characteristically examined questions such as the nature of bravery, the justification of war, and why men serve. "The Wood-felling" was less altered by the censor and elicited this encouragement from Nekrasov, editor of *Sovremennik:* "Do not neglect such sketches; our literature has so far said nothing about the soldier except vulgar trivialities" (2:408). In a digression about the character of the true Russian soldier, Tolstoy had singled out such traits as "modesty, simplicity, and the capacity for seeing in danger something quite different from the danger itself."

I have seen a soldier wounded in the leg who at first regretted only the hole in his new sheepskin coat. . . . Who does not remember the incident at the siege of Gergebel when the fuse of a loaded bomb caught fire in the laboratory and a sergeant ordered two soldiers to take the bomb and run to throw it into a ditch, and how the soldiers did not throw it into the closest place near the colonel's tent, which stood above the ditch, but carried it further so as not to awaken the gentlemen who were resting in the tent, and both were blown to bits. (2:83)

Behind the admiration for such selfless heroism looms a disturbing uncertainty about its value, especially when the stakes are as low as a new coat or a gentleman's rest. Tolstoy resolved the question quite conclusively in his three *Sevastopol Stories,* based upon his own experiences in the Crimean War, published in 1855–56.

The first story, "Sevastopol in December," is a grimly inspiring description of the Russian soldiers defending the city, and such things as their makeshift hospital and the notoriously dangerous Fourth Bastion. Tolstoy characteristically insists that no matter what you have heard about the war beforehand, you will not be prepared for what you find there. Typical also is the account of a sailor who, though gravely wounded, asks the stretcher-bearers to stop so that he can watch the Russians' cannon fire. Though incapacitated, he wants to return to the Bastion to help train the younger men. The Russian people, Tolstoy concludes, are "the hero" of his tale (2:101). It would not be surprising if Alexander II did order his commanders to safeguard the life of its young author, as was later rumored.

The last two *Sevastopol Stories,* however, reflect Tolstoy's bitter disillusionment with the war: his hero was now, as he announced at the end of "Sevastopol in May," "truth." Understandably, the censor cut from the text numerous insinuations that the Russian officers were pampered cowards, greedy for personal glory. Even so, the published versions of these stories reflect Tolstoy's sad conviction that even the bravest men were dying in vain. As the Russians are finally forced to abandon Sevastopol, one soldier concludes: "How many of our men are dead, and for nothing—the French got it anyway!"(2:205).

The *Sevastopol Stories* clearly anticipate Tolstoy's belief, voiced repeatedly in *War and Peace,* that the course of war is quite arbitrary, depending less on the strategies of generals than on the spontaneous actions of individual soldiers in the front lines. One example is the death of Praskukhin, an episode R. F. Christian has termed "one of Tolstoy's early artistic triumphs." Praskukhin's comrade Mikhailov, Christian observes, "who is unharmed by the shell which kills his neighbor, thinks *he* has been killed, while its victim, Praskukhin, believes he is only wounded—a situation deliberately in keeping with the author's ironical approach to war and his assumption that it is not what it appears to be."[3]

The live shell that spins between Mikhailov and Praskukhin before exploding also anticipates the episode in *War and Peace* when Prince Andrew is critically wounded. Here, Praskukhin's remarkable inner monologue contains three of the stages found to occur in what—a century later—would be known as NDE's, or near-death experiences. As the shell spins, Praskukhin first experiences "denial" ("perhaps Mikhailov alone will be killed"); then a vivid "life review" containing some oddly irrelevant details (a gypsy melody he had sung, a woman he had loved wearing her lilac bonnet); and, finally, "acceptance" ("he stretched himself out, and no longer did he see, hear, think or feel"). We then read: "He had been killed on the spot by a bomb splinter in the center of his chest" (2:134). This comes as something of a shock, since Praskukhin's inner monologue takes up most of two pages, but his thoughts seem totally realistic and aptly convey the vivid compression of a near-death experience.

In "Sevastopol in May," Tolstoy twice views the effects of war through the eyes of children. First, a ten-year-old girl marvels at the shooting stars in the sky, asking why there are so many (2:119). Later, a ten-year-old boy wanders "with vacant curiosity" among the corpses, picking flowers. Having gathered a large bouquet, he holds his nose because of the odor carried to him by the wind. Then, after staring long at a "horrible headless body" and repeatedly touching its stiffly outstretched, resilient arm with his foot, the boy suddenly screams, hides his face in the flowers, and runs away as fast as possible (2:144).

In this second instance of "making strange," the ironic contrast between the flowers and the stench of the corpses renders the latter especially repulsive. In "Sevastopol in August," Tolstoy employed an
intensified form of "making strange" by having a nurse at the field
hospital react to the horror of a young soldier who stares at the wounded with agonized sympathy, repeating, "Oh, my God!" Realizing that
the young man has himself just arrived, the nurse exclaims in turn:
"My God, my God! When will it all end!" (2:171) Tolstoy concludes
his condemnation of the war by stressing the "remorse, shame and
malice" felt by the retreating soldiers and the desire for self-preservation that is "present in the soul of each one" (2:207).

Living for Others

In *Semeinoe schastie* (*Family Happiness*), a short novel published in
1859, Tolstoy focuses first upon the emotional blossoming of a young
woman, then upon the decline of romantic love within the framework
of marriage and society. The narrator is a woman upon whom the author imposes his own views. In fact, the novel is based on Tolstoy's
own courtship of Valerya Arseneva three years before, and can be read
as a rather moralistic projection of that relationship. However, the
young woman's thoughts and feelings are delicately rendered.

Seventeen-year-old Masha, in mourning for her mother, is visited by
Sergey Mikhailich, thirty-six, a friend of her deceased father. He seems
to lack the solemn sadness of her other visitors: "at first this indiffer-
ence seemed strange and even improper on the part of a close friend.
But then I understood that this was not indifference, but sincerity, and
I was grateful for it" (3:74).

When Sergey Mikhailich returns a few months later, Masha is puzzled by "his complete indifference and even contempt for my appearance. . . . However, I soon understood what he needed. He wanted to
believe that there was no coquettishness in me" (3:83). The pattern is
thus familiar: a puzzling indifference that seems to shade into something worse is soon understood as a respect for the sincere and natural.
But this time, Masha recalls, she became *affectedly* simple: she was not
yet able to be naturally so.

The young girl nevertheless tries to learn from Sergey Mikhailich:
"Not without good reason did he say that the only sure happiness in

life is—to live for another" (3:85). Although this seemed "strange" and she did not "understand" it, she adds, it became a conviction of hers. The two of them soon fall in love, and Masha is inspired to give charity, anonymously, to a peasant forced to beg for the wood to build a coffin for his daughter. After this she fully "understands" what had seemed "strange" in Sergey Mikhailich: "Only now did I understand why he had said that to live for another is the only happiness, and I completely agreed with him" (3:99).

After their marriage, however, the goal of "living for another" proves elusive: contrary to her expectations, "there was merely a selfish feeling of love for each other, the desire to be loved" (3:111). Masha enters the social round and drifts apart from her husband. Only in the novel's closing paragraph do we learn that after romance had passed, she felt a new love for her husband and children, which marked the beginning of her present happiness—a "happiness" that anticipates in its narrowness the situation of Natasha in the first epilogue to *War and Peace.*

The Cossacks (1863), an autobiographical tale of a young nobleman's experiences in the Caucasus, further explores the theory that happiness derives from living for others. Tolstoy wrestled with the novel for ten years without being satisfied by it. Its plot has been likened to *The Gypsies* and contrasted with *The Prisoner of the Caucasus,* both long poems by Pushkin.[4] *The Cossacks* is a mature and complex work that has been variously interpreted. D. S. Mirsky has suggested that it is Tolstoy's "masterpiece before *War and Peace.*" In his opinion the Cossacks, despite all their killing, fornicating, and stealing, are "hopelessly superior" in their natural beauty to the nobleman Olenin, who is "much more moral, but civilized and consequently contaminated."[5] However, as R. F. Christian has observed, "The Cossack way of life is not held up as an answer to Olenin's problems."[6] Indeed, social values are carefully balanced against natural ones in the story, and both are found lacking.

As the novel opens Olenin is leaving Moscow for the Caucasus, where he hopes to begin a new life. Nearing the Caucasus, Olenin vividly imagines a beautiful native girl among the mountains; and after he meets Maryanka upon arrival, she and the mountains are repeatedly mentioned together. The association is apt: he finds her beautiful, natural, cold, and inaccessible. Olenin befriends a white-haired Herculean hunter named Eroshka, who preaches the pleasures of free love and offers girls for wine. Olenin soon prefers Maryanka, though she intends to marry the brave young Lukashka. Maryanka wavers. When Lukashka is critically wounded, she coldly rejects Olenin.

The story is carefully patterned, and contains what appear to be fateful themes and fateful parallel constructions. The frequent association of Maryanka with the mountains, for example, culminates in Olenin's statement: "I loved to look at her beauty, like the beauty of the mountains and the sky . . ." (3:271). And: "Perhaps in her I love nature . . . but I do not have my own will; some kind of elemental force loves her through me . . ." (3:273).

While drinking wine with Olenin, Eroshka watches moths flying into a candle flame. "Fool, fool!" he exclaims. "You're destroying your own self, and I pity you" (3:208). At the end of the novel they again drink, and as Olenin departs, Eroshka exclaims: "Fool! fool! . . . I pity you so!" Like a "piteous" moth, Olenin has been "destroying his own self," flying blindly into the flame of his love for Maryanka.

Eroshka tells Lukashka: "Trusting is all right, but don't go to sleep without a gun" (3:213), and Lukashka listens to him "attentively." Lukashka's dumb sister (a Tolstoyan "unlikely prophet") then signals to him by using her hand as an imaginary gun that he must kill another Chechen (3:216). While trying to capture a Chechen alive, Lukashka is critically wounded.

We do not know Lukashka's fate, but a pattern suggests that he will survive. Eroshka had been the "foremost brave lad" (*pervyi molodets*) of the village (3:209), a description that fits Lukashka perfectly. Moreover, Eroshka says of Lukashka: "I love him. I was just like that myself" (3:221). When Lukashka is critically wounded, Eroshka recalls that he himself had been gravely wounded, but he drank himself into a stupor and survived (3:298). And of Lukashka, he reports: "vodka is all his soul accepts. . . . He was a fine young fellow, a warrior like I was. I too lay dying like that . . ." (3:299).

Midway through the novel Olenin is completely covered with mosquitoes while out hunting. He overcomes his first impulse to run away and tries to tolerate them. Then the mosquitoes become an integral part of the natural setting, and "he found pleasant precisely that which had seemed terrible and intolerable" (3:226). Olenin lies down and undergoes a Tolstoyan fateful change in attitude: with the sun standing directly overhead, he suddenly has "a strange feeling of causeless happiness and love for everything." His consciousness first narrows (he even likens himself to a mosquito) then expands in a burst of clarity as he realizes that "happiness consists in living for others." Returning to the village, Olenin gives his rival Lukashka a horse. The Cossacks, accustomed to doing favors only in exchange for something else, misinterpret the gift, ascribing sinister motives to Olenin. In short, his theory fails so completely that he eventually regards his attempt at self-renunciation as "all pride" (3:274).

Chapter Four
War and Peace

Tolstoy's longest and perhaps greatest novel underwent several false starts and numerous revisions. Behind it lay two intentions. For many years Tolstoy had wished to write an accurate account of early nineteenth-century European history, and so decided to write about a man returning in 1856 from exile in Siberia after taking part in the abortive Decembrist uprising of 1825. As he explained in an unpublished foreword to the beginning of the novel, he soon found it necessary to trace his hero back to 1805, and the first thirty-eight chapters appeared in early 1865, in the *Russian Messenger,* under the title *1805.* A year later, Tolstoy wrote Fet that he hoped to finish the work by 1867 and publish it under the title *All's Well That Ends Well.*[1] He made so many changes, though, that the last chapters appeared only in 1869.

War and Peace is first of all a celebration of life. In this work more than any other, Tolstoy succeeded in achieving what he termed (in a famous unposted letter of July-August, 1865) "the aim of an artist": "to make people love life in all its countless inexhaustible manifestations."[2] An astonishing multitude of vividly individualized characters promotes this end; even the dogs, as the critic Nikolay Strakhov noted, are individualized.[3] The novel also provides a patriotic view of Russian history beginning in 1805 and extending beyond Napoleon's invasion of 1812, seen through a very special lens of Tolstoyan determinism. In some respects, it is a heroic epic in the tradition of Homer's *Iliad.*[4] Though the historical sections of *War and Peace* are successfully interrelated with the fictional ones, the work sprawls so idiosyncratically as to cause Henry James to label it a "loose baggy monster."[5]

Tolstoy anticipated objections to the form of his work. "What is *War and Peace?*" he proleptically addressed its first readers. "It is not a novel, still less an epic poem, still less an historical chronicle. *War and Peace* is that which the author wished to and could express in that form in which it found expression."[6] Tolstoy repeatedly insisted that the best works of Russian literature had their own unique and necessary form. And there was considerable truth in this: Pushkin's masterpiece *Eugene*

Onegin is subtitled "a novel in verse"; Gogol's great novel *Dead Souls* is subtitled "an epic poem"; Lermontov's novel *A Hero of Our Time* consists of five separate but interconnected stories; and so on.

Who is the hero of *War and Peace?* Here too there can be no easy answer. A good case can be made for the Russian people, or for Russia itself. More narrowly, the hero of Tolstoy's novel has been considered a combination of Prince Andrew and Pierre, as two sides of the author himself, or even tripartite person (including Nicholas). Yet we should not forget Natasha, a central figure intimately related to the other main characters. One critic has even seen *War and Peace* as "a gigantic novel of education, centering not on one protagonist but on five" (the above four plus Princess Mary).[7] Another critic, after naming these five, contends that none of them is "the hero" of the novel, which is deliberately "decentralized" in order to create an illusion of the essence of life.[8] However, if one looks for "a hero and a heroine," Pierre and Natasha stand out for a variety of reasons.

Pierre and Natasha

The impishly enchanting Natasha was generally modeled upon Tolstoy's younger sister-in-law, and in many respects the kindly, bearlike Pierre recalls Tolstoy himself. It is they who celebrate life the most fully in *War and Peace* and most strikingly display a virtue that may be termed spontaneous altruism. Moreover, Pierre and Natasha are linked by numerous similar traits, attitudes, and circumstances long before they come together at the end of the novel.

To begin with, each is disastrously involved with a Kuragin. Pierre's marriage to Hélène almost results in his death (in a duel with Dolokhov); Natasha's infatuation with Anatole almost results in her death (by suicide). Both amorous involvements are officially "engineered" by Kuragins, Prince Vasily and Hélène. Also, Dolokhov causes evil behind the scenes of both relationships, as Hélène's presumed lover and as Anatole's resourceful accomplice. Both Pierre and Natasha initially wonder if their infatuations are somehow wrong, after which they rather strangely yield to the Kuragins: Pierre tells himself that his marriage to Hélène is predestined (4:260); Natasha rationalizes that Hélène's good husband Pierre probably approves of her involvement with Anatole (5:351). Moreover, both amorous involvements are appropriately punctuated by exclamations in the French language. When Pierre submits to Hélène, he rather awkwardly blurts out *"Je vous aime!"* (4:270). When Anatole singles out Natasha, he exclaims *"Mais charmante!"* (5:339). As R. F. Christian has observed, the use of French "of or by a Russian" in *War and Peace* "very often has a suggestion of sophistication, artificiality, even mendacity."[9] This falsity is appropriately reflected by the backgrounds of each episode. Hélène's parents wait impatiently for Pierre to propose, spying on him and finally pressuring him into it. Natasha and Anatole are attracted to each other against a backdrop of opera which travesties his intended abduction of her[10] and which is deliberately rendered artificial by Tolstoy's technique of "making strange." This Gallicized falsity contrasts with the normally natural Russianness of both Natasha and Pierre. Natasha's natural Russianness is repeatedly emphasized when she does a Russian dance (5:227); Pierre's, when he decides that he is predestined to kill Napoleon (6:371–72).

Pierre and Natasha succumb in similar ways: both are startled by the "terrible nearness" of the Kuragins, and both feel that protective "barriers" have been removed (4:260, 261; 5:343). After Pierre's duel, when Hélène viciously insults him, he is likened to "a hare, surrounded by dogs, who lays back its ears and continues to crouch down before its enemies" (5:35). When Natasha, after failing to elope with Anatole, learns that he was already married, she is likened to "a wounded, cornered animal who looks at the approaching dogs and hunters" (5:377).

The "natural, Russian" Natasha and Pierre thus give in to the "false, French" Kuragins, but after much suffering they both emerge somehow stronger and ready to rebuild their lives. This process recapitulates in miniature the abandonment of Moscow to the French Army, a decision so inevitable, Tolstoy insists, that "every Russian" might have predicted it (6:288). In all three cases, Tolstoy's imagery is aptly similar. At great length, Tolstoy likens the burned, abandoned city of Moscow to a bee hive charred and cleansed by fire (6:340–42). At the end of the novel, Natasha declares that Pierre has been morally cleansed as if by a steam bath (7:236), and he too finds a great change in her, barely recognizing the woman in a black dress with dark eyes and a thin, pale, stern face (7:227–28). In all three cases, the imagery has a remarkably positive aspect. The stern woman in the black dress seems "dear, kind, marvelous" and even "kindred" to Pierre; Natasha finds Pierre "pure, smooth, fresh" after his moral steam bath; the charred ruins of Moscow "astonish" Pierre with their "beauty" (7:239).

Natasha and Pierre are uniquely similar in their combination of sensitivity, spontaneity, altruism, and effectiveness. Indeed, the most significant similarity between them is their readiness to help people in distress. However, Pierre displays the quality of spontaneous altruism only after considerable Tolstoyan searching, whereas Natasha exhibits it from the very first. Early in the novel, for example, when Sonya bursts into tears because Vera has said unkind things about her, Natasha immediately embraces, comforts, and kisses her. Sonya brightens up with shining eyes, like a kitten ready to play again (4:86). Natasha displays the spontaneous ability to console others most fully when Petya dies and she quite literally comforts her mother back to life, supporting the almost insanely aggrieved woman with healing love and tenderness for three days and nights.

Perhaps still more remarkable is the selfless efficiency with which Natasha works to help others. When her mother cruelly accuses Sonya of ingratitude and of scheming to catch Nicholas, relations between those three become almost unbearably strained. However, we learn from a one-sentence paragraph that Natasha set to work to bring about a reconciliation and succeeded admirably (5:303). Most striking of all, though, is what Natasha accomplishes during the evacuation of Moscow. First, she arranges for some of the wounded soldiers to stay in the Rostovs' house. Then it is Natasha alone who blocks the monstrous decision to cart away household goods when the wounded could be taken instead. The servants, we are told, crowd around Natasha, unable to believe her strange instructions, but soon they joyously and energetically work to transport the wounded soldiers, and it all seems not strange to them now, but inevitable (6:327).

After Pierre becomes a Freemason, he gives large sums of money to their cause and tells Prince Andrew: "only now, when I live, at least, when I try to live (Pierre modestly corrected himself) for others, only now do I understand all the happiness of life" (5:117). This formulation resembles earlier ones to be found in Tolstoy's works—for example, in *A Landowner's Morning* and *The Cossacks*—with one qualification: Pierre's modest correction suggests that his happiness in helping others is less self-centered than Nekhlyudov's or Olenin's. Pierre thus draws closer to answering the Tolstoyan question of how we should live. Though Prince Andrew replies, "Yes, if only it were so!"—we then learn that he has now begun "a new inner life" (5:124).

After Natasha, failing to elope with Anatole, has attempted suicide, Pierre talks with her, and she is suddenly struck by his "timid, tender, heart-felt" voice (5:387). He then warmly offers her his friendship and

sympathy. Natasha declares herself unworthy, and Pierre is himself
amazed at his next words: "If I were not myself, but the handsomest,
most intelligent and best man in the world, and if I were free, I would
this very moment ask on my knees for your hand and your love!" Natasha sheds "tears of gratitude and tenderness," and it is clear that
Pierre's spontaneous generosity has set her recovery in motion. Pierre
later saves an enemy officer, protects an Armenian girl, and rescues a
child from the Moscow fire; these acts parallel Natasha's efficient helping of the wounded soldiers. Together, Pierre and Natasha display a
greater degree of spontaneous altruism than any other principal characters in Tolstoy's works, with the possible exception of Kitty in *Anna
Karenina*.

From the very beginning of the novel, Pierre and Natasha are associated by suggestions of childhood and fairy tale–like pleasure. During
the opening soiree scene Pierre is likened to "a child in a toyshop," and
we first see Natasha at age thirteen when she rushes recklessly in with
her doll. She then hides in the conservatory "as if under a cap of invis-
ibility," a Russian fairy-tale image; Pierre soon pretends to be Napoleon, piercing an "invisible" enemy with his sword.

In their childlike enthusiasm, both are inspired to emulate others
early in the novel. When Dolokhov, for a bet, drains an entire bottle
of rum while precariously balanced on a window ledge, Pierre watches
like a frightened child. His expression combines a faint smile of excitement with terror and fear: "Why is it so long?" he wonders. "It
seemed to him that more than half an hour had gone by." Pierre twice
averts his eyes, the second time telling himself "that he would never
open them again." But when he does, and sees that Dolokhov has won,
Pierre insists on emulating him, even without a bet. "I'll do it! Bring
me a bottle!" he repeatedly shouts.

Also early in the novel, Natasha hides in the Rostovs' conservatory,
pleased that Boris is looking for her. At this point Nicholas and Sonya
(who is jealous and upset at him) meet nearby, and Natasha excitedly
eavesdrops upon their reconciliation. Sonya sobs, and Nicholas takes
her hand: "Natasha, not stirring and not breathing, watched from her
hiding place with shining eyes. 'What will happen now?' she wondered." Nicholas asks Sonya's forgiveness and kisses her: "Oh, how
nice!" Natasha thinks. When they leave, she calls Boris to her "with a
meaningful and sly expression" and proposes that he kiss her doll. He
hesitates. Natasha's flushed face expresses both triumph and fear:

"'And would you like to kiss me?' she whispered almost inaudibly, looking up at him from under her eyebrows, smiling, and almost crying from excitement." When Boris still hesitates Natasha jumps up on a tub and kisses him full upon the lips. As the scene ends, she counts on her fingers the years remaining until she will be sixteen and Boris can ask for her hand in marriage.

During this entire episode, Natasha seems disarmingly innocent. Her conduct is hardly above reproach—she spies upon two lovers and makes bold advances to Boris—and yet the childlike wonder with which she looks on ("What will happen now?") and her joy at the lovers' reconciliation ("Oh, how nice!") render her slyness forgivable, and even quite appealing. As in the episode with Pierre and Dolokhov, life is seen as an exciting game to play and to experience fully. Both Pierre and Natasha are anxious at whatever cost to experience the intensity of what they have just witnessed. Both display a compelling desire to plunge into the tide of life.

The intensity of Natasha's and Pierre's experiences is indirectly— but all the more powerfully—conveyed by the momentary impairment of their sight and hearing. Thus after Pierre's confrontation with Hélène, he "did not hear and did not see anything" (5:69); and when he tries to kill Napoleon, "he did not hear anything and did not see anything around himself" (6:403). When Natasha learns that Petya has been killed she "did not see, did not hear" (7:187); as she enters the ballroom at her first ball, "the steady hum of voices, footsteps, and greetings deafened Natasha; the light and glitter blinded her still more" (5:207).

The intensity of the immediate experience is irresistible: early in the novel both Pierre and Natasha give their "word of honor" only to break it later. First, Pierre emphatically gives Andrew his word not to go to Anatole Kuragin's (4:41), then recalls that he had already promised Anatole. Besides, he reasons, "words of honor" are "conventional things with no definite meaning, especially if one considers that by tomorrow he may have died"—and goes anyway. Natasha gives her "word of honor" not to tell anyone that Nicholas has been wounded— and immediately rushes to tell Sonya about it (4:295). Upon seeing Sonya's reaction, however, Natasha embraces her, bursts into tears, and explains that Nicholas, only slightly wounded, writes that he is "now well" and promoted to the rank of officer.

Especially as viewed against the backdrop of apparently predestined historical events in *War and Peace,* Natasha's and Pierre's parallel circumstances tend to suggest that they are fatefully related. Early in the novel Natasha, still aglow after kissing Boris, sits opposite Pierre at dinner. Her glance, filled with love for Boris, sometimes rests on Pierre: "and the look of this funny, animated girl made him want to laugh without knowing why" (4:80). Soon thereafter, Natasha herself exclaims: "that fat Pierre who sat opposite me is so funny!" (4:86). "How happy I feel!" she adds. Much later, at the Bergs' party, we learn that Pierre "happened to sit opposite Natasha" (5:224) when she has just fallen in love with Prince Andrew. "What has happened to her?" Pierre wonders. These parallels seem still more fateful after Natasha becomes engaged to Prince Andrew: "Pierre was avoiding Natasha. It seemed to him that his feeling for her was stronger than a married man's should be for his friend's fiancée. And some kind of fate continually brought him together with her" (5:374).

Long before Pierre realizes that he loves Natasha, he is uniquely sensitive to her feelings, and she to his. After Pierre's duel with Dolokhov, everyone in the Rostov house likes Dolokhov except Natasha, who "insisted that he was an evil person, that in the duel with Bezukhov, Pierre was right and Dolokhov was guilty, that he was unpleasant and unnatural" (5:48). Talking with her mother at night, Natasha then reveals a deeper affection for Pierre than perhaps she consciously realizes. Having playfully dismissed Boris as "narrow" and "grey," Natasha abruptly declares that Pierre is "dark blue with red" (5:201). Her mother, laughing, remarks that Natasha flirts with Pierre too, but Natasha denies it, insisting that Pierre is a "fine" person, "dark blue with red."

Since Pierre and Natasha are associated from the first in a separate dimension of childlike enthusiasm and imagination, it is appropriate that she here reveals a preference for him in what appears to be a rather silly game of childlike perception. Natasha's ostensibly playful notion of "red with blue" is mysteriously echoed by Sonya in a game of predicting the future. First, Sonya pretends to see Prince Andrew "lying down" with a "happy" expression, thus unwittingly predicting the circumstances of his death. Asked what came afterwards, Sonya replies: "something blue and red" (5:301). She therefore becomes one of Tolstoy's most remarkable unlikely prophets by also predicting Natasha's marriage to Pierre. The "red and blue" prediction was obviously important to Tolstoy, for Natasha and Sonya discuss it much later, confusing the details but marveling at its accuracy (7:37–38).

Andrew

If Pierre and Natasha embody an intense celebration of life, Prince Andrew suggests by indirection a cyclical affirmation of the life force. From the beginning he is pointedly contrasted with his close friend Pierre. Andrew, we are told, "combined in the highest degree all those qualities which Pierre lacked and which can best be expressed by the concept, strength of will" (4:40). Pierre admires Andrew's self-control and is astonished by his capacity for work and study. Later, we learn that Andrew's stern father (modeled on Tolstoy's maternal grandfather) recognizes only two virtues: activity and intellect. His sister Mary, however, accuses Andrew of "a kind of intellectual pride" (4:136).

If we return to the distinction Tolstoy made when he was writing *Childhood* between "from the head" and "from the heart," we will recall that he preferred the latter, despite its apparent crudeness. We may therefore suspect that Andrew's cool intellect and strength of will, so generously envied by warm-hearted Pierre, are, in a sense, weaknesses masquerading as strengths. This is by no means clear at first: Pierre's naïveté and rather irresponsible naturalness seem to contrast quite unfavorably with Andrew's sophisticated self-control. Yet for this very reason, Pierre is more open to personal development, especially since he lives more by the heart than by the head. Their attitudes toward Napoleon provide a revealing contrast: Pierre imagines himself to be Napoleon in a make-believe game; Andrew admires Napoleon as a master military strategist. Pierre's character, Tolstoy suggests, is not yet formed (4:42), whereas Andrew's, in taking shape, has acquired a hard surface crust; for most of his life he is enviably protected from other people, but also sadly isolated from them. Prince Andrew easily sees through others (at least, enough for his own purposes), but until he is mortally wounded he lacks the capacity for a full and open relationship with others that would necessarily render him somewhat vulnerable.

Primarily for these reasons, Andrew, throughout the novel, remains oddly static. Each lesson he learns leaves him in need of another. Each time his protective surface crust is penetrated—whether by loss or by love—it seems to close over once again. John Hagan has observed that Prince Andrew goes through "five distinct cycles of death and rebirth," arranged "so that what is metaphorical in the first four becomes literal reality in the fifth."[11] The first cycle, Hagan suggests, begins with Andrew's fall at the battle of Austerlitz (his wound is described as if it were mortal, and Andrew's father tells everyone that his son is dead).

Andrew's prior conceptions of Napoleon and military glory "die" at this point, yet he also discovers "peace" in the lofty, infinite sky, which suggests a "rebirth." The second cycle commences with his wife Lise's death, when Andrew's guilt causes "a second spiritual death of his own." This time, Hagan finds, the rebirth consists of two parts: Andrew's brief turning to God (in his conversation with Pierre at the ferry) and his turning to Nature and Natasha (climaxed by the nocturnal window scene at Otradnoe). The famous old oak mirrors Andrew's feeling that life is over, and then his regeneration when he observes its transformation. Cycle three begins with Andrew's "fatal" involvement with the rationalist Speransky and ends with a new, stronger feeling of love for Natasha and his proposal of marriage. She then begins cycle four by attempting to elope with Anatole; it ends with Andrew's vigorous condemnation of war in conversation with Pierre before the battle of Borodino. In the fifth cycle Andrew literally dies, but does so with the conviction that "death is an awakening."

It should be noted that the first two cycles are composed of what Tolstoy terms at one point the "best moments" of Andrew's life. Upon seeing that the bare old oak at Otradnoe has suddenly become gloriously green, Andrew recalls these "best" moments: "Austerlitz with that lofty sky, his wife's dead, reproachful face, Pierre at the ferry, and that girl thrilled by the beauty of the night, and that night, and the moon" (5:165). The first of these four moments comprises the entire first cycle; the last three, the composite second one. How, we may wonder, can Lise's dead reproachful face constitute a "best" moment? Moreover, would Tolstoy have considered the main elements of the last three cycles—including the painful blow of Natasha's attempted elopement—to be Andrew's best moments as well?

In attempting to answer the first question, Edward Wasiolek has observed that Lise's reproachful face causes Andrew to understand for the first time "that he has violated by his judgment the sacredness of her being."[12] Wasiolek notes that the other three moments involve the sky, which reminds Andrew that "life within him is infinite" as he "catches a glimpse of something that is not circumscribed by his understanding." The connection is thus the fact that Andrew senses the limitations of his intellect during each moment. All this is helpful, but the crucial criterion of a "best" moment seems to be that a period of heightened consciousness—no matter how disillusioning or painful—leads to positive personal growth. Moreover, Prince Andrew's four moments of growth seem still more unified if we return once again to

Tolstoy's distinction between the head and the heart. During the first two moments Andrew realizes, at least briefly, the danger of living "from the head." He realizes that his intensely rational approach (to Napoleon, military glory, and his own wife) is inadequate and wrong. During the last two moments, Andrew recognizes the importance of living "from the heart." His turning to God with Pierre at the ferry leads him to begin "a new inner life," and his turning to Nature, inspired by Natasha's joyful enthusiasm at the window, reinforces this internal rebirth. All four moments, however ostensibly disparate, form two halves of a consistent, unified process of personal growth. Andrew's longstanding and all-consuming commitment to living from the head, however, renders this growth incomplete for most, if not all, of his life.

We may now attempt to answer the question about Andrew's other "best" moments. Cycle three (his disenchantment with the rationalist Speransky and his increased love for Natasha) clearly fits the pattern of movement from the head toward the heart. The end of the fourth cycle—Andrew's condemnation of war—aptly echoes the end of cycle one. The beginning of cycle four, Natasha's attempted elopement, is far less obviously a "best" moment, yet in a very real sense this echoes the beginning of cycle two: by agreeing to postpone his engagement to Natasha, Andrew treats her in much the same coldly rational way that he did Lise. Wasiolek goes so far as to insist that it is not Natasha who betrays Andrew, but he her,[13] and there is some truth in this. Still, if Natasha's attempted elopement is to be a "best" moment for Andrew, he must realize his error sufficiently to achieve significant personal growth—and this he never quite seems to do. Not long before his death, Andrew derives "comfort" from thinking that "love is God" and that as a particle of love, he will, at death, return to the eternal source. "But," as Tolstoy rather pointedly remarks, "these were only thoughts" (7:69). Andrew, we may infer, still lives too much from the head. Finally, however, a "veil" that has obscured Andrew's "spiritual vision" is lifted: his last days are "an awakening from life," and he realizes that "death is an awakening."

Apart from the concepts of "cycles" and "best moments," Andrew may be profitably seen also in terms of his relationship to Pierre. The goal of "living for oneself" that Andrew expounds to Pierre contrasts sharply with the latter's answer about "living for others" (5:117). It is therefore rather ironic that Andrew in fact carries out with great efficiency all the reforms that Pierre vainly attempts on his estates (5:159–

60). Andrew's advice to Pierre ("don't marry, my friend, don't marry!" [4:40]) is ironically echoed by Pierre's advice to Andrew that he "marry, marry, marry" Natasha (5:230). And this is part of another symmetry: each friend (with far-reaching results) directs the other toward Natasha. Pierre urges Andrew to ask Natasha to dance (5:211); Andrew brings Pierre to Natasha and tells her to rely on him alone (5:238–39).

Prince Andrew is framed by a window or a door at several crucial moments of his life.[14] Important episodes featuring doors and windows associate Andrew with life and death—and, symmetrically, with Pierre. Early in the novel, they are both excited by episodes at open windows: Pierre, by Dolokhov and the rum bottle; Andrew, by Natasha and the beautiful night. Whereas Pierre is inspired to defy death, Andrew is inspired to begin a new life. Tolstoy eventually uses the image of a shattering window to describe the exploding shell that fatally wounds Prince Andrew (6:262). Much earlier, when Andrew returns to his wife, Lise, a strong wind blows out a candle through a window, in a prefiguration of her death (5:43). Someone later holds a door shut against him as his son is born. Hagan has related this door, behind which struggle life and death, to the door through which Andrew's own death later seems to force itself.[15] That door, which exists only in a dream resembling a vision and admits Andrew's death, may be linked to the metaphorical door that seems to open on rusty hinges when Pierre is finally united with Natasha to begin a new life (7:228).

War and Peace with Women

Anna Mikhailovna is said to "conquer" a position next to Prince Vasily as she fights for Boris's advancement (4:67), and she literally engages in a tug of war with Catiche for the old Count Bezukhov's portfolio. As Anna Pavlovna maneuvers Pierre into desiring Hélène, she is said to be "in the excited condition of a commander on a battlefield" (4:258). And when Anatole arrives at Bald Hills, Andrew's pregnant wife, Lise, "like an old war horse that hears the trumpet, unconsciously and forgetting her condition, prepared for the accustomed gallop of coquetry" (4:286).

Tolstoy was not kind to women in *War and Peace*. "Selfish, vain, stupid, trivial in every way—that's women when you see them as they really are," Andrew tells Pierre (4:40). "Women are especially harmful," Dolokhov tells Nicholas, "countesses or cooks, it's all the same—I have yet to meet a woman who was not a creature for sale" (5:47–

48). Vera is spiteful; Hélène is both superficial and predatory. Julie Karagina debases love through calculation: for example, there is something tendentiously despicable about the way Julie's face gleams "with triumph and self-satisfaction" as she forces her fiancé, Boris, to vow "that he loved her and had never loved any woman more than her. She knew that for the Penza estates and the Nizhegorod forests she could demand this, and she got what she demanded" (5:326).

Natasha, on the other hand, is a truly delightful heroine, at least until the epilogue. Charmingly spontaneous and generous, she enlivens all those with whom she comes into contact. Her enthusiastic love of life helps others even when she is not aware of their presence: thus when Prince Andrew overhears her rapturous exclamations at the window about the beauty of the night, his despair gives way to a host of youthful thoughts and hopes arising in his soul. Natasha can melt the layers of pride and cynicism Andrew has built around himself. Even after her attempted elopement, he recalls "that spiritual force [of hers], that sincerity, that openness of soul" (6:220).

Yet when we meet her in the epilogue, after seven years of marriage to Pierre, we find a very different Natasha. Now "stouter and broader" (7:278), she neglects her hair and her clothing. She has purposely abandoned all her enchanting ways, including her singing, precisely because they were seductive. Here one may cite from *Family Happiness* Sergey Mikhailich's instructing Masha in the "undesirability" of coquettishness, and from *Anna Karenina* Levin's squirming with painful embarrassment when he sits opposite a girl who wears a low-cut dress for his benefit.

Having eradicated her sparkling charm, Natasha now centers her entire being upon her family: "her husband, whom she had to hold so that he would belong undividedly to her and to the home—and the children, who had to be carried, born, nursed, and brought up." Natasha's jealousy is a common object of family amusement. She strictly controls Pierre, who dares not even smile when he talks with another woman. In return, Natasha places herself "on a footing of slave to her husband." She tries to anticipate his every wish, yet she uses his own words against him if he seems to be changing his mind. Pierre's "joyous" sense of his own identity as "not a bad man" results from "seeing himself reflected in his wife" (7:282).

Unattractive as this mutual absorption and mutual enslavement may appear, it is an almost inevitable development of what Tolstoy then considered a highly satisfactory marriage. For him, a good wife was nurturing and supportive, yet constraining and somehow sexless. Ruth Benson puts it, "Tolstoy's own and his heroes' search for moral purity" were "constantly threatened" by "woman's selfish interests and particularly her sexuality."[16] Only total absorption in marriage and family could disarm the dangerous weapon of female sexuality. The more earthy vitality a young girl radiated, the more necessary it was that she be quickly herded into the safe confines of family life.

The young Natasha fairly bursts with undirected energy. Significantly, she is called "gunpowder" early in the novel (4:56). As her performance of a Russian peasant dance pointedly suggests, society had failed to squelch in her that primitive force of nature which is not separate from female sexual energy. Hence, grave danger: the same capacity for total abandonment makes Natasha susceptible to the depravity of the Kuragins—which in turn leads to her suicide attempt. As Barabara Monter has observed of Anna Karenina: "Anna's vitality, the essence of her attractiveness, is made up in large part of sexuality, and with Tolstoj sexuality fulfills only itself and leads away from life. Thus we have the paradox of Anna who is so alive ending in suicide."[17]

Natasha's realization of her near doom and of the value of the man she has abandoned tames her sensuality, as does her association with that spiritually elevated, Tolstoyan wife and mother, Princess Mary. Nevertheless, her transformation in the epilogue is quite startling and rather tendentious. Tolstoy remarks that only the old countess understood the change: she "knew by her maternal insight that all Natasha's bursts of impulsiveness had their origin merely in the need of having a family, of having a husband" (7:278). After Natasha's marriage, her face has "none of the ever-burning fire of animation that had formerly constituted its charm," and she withdraws from society, which finds her "neither attractive nor amiable."

Tolstoy's treatment of Natasha reflects Russian religious and social tradition. Before Peter the Great initiated the custom of having upper-class women appear at court and social functions, they were severely restricted, spending their entire lives in separate, prisonlike quarters called the *terem*. Still earlier, Byzantine Christianity had brought to Russia a dual image of woman: Mary the Virgin Mother and Eve the temptress. The concept of sex as sin carried over into marriage. The icons had to be covered during marital relations, and ablutions had to be performed afterwards. The popular "Parable of Feminine Evil" by the Byzantine church father St. John Chrysostom described women as "insinuating, cunning, stealthy; slanderers, ensnarers, heretics, wolverines, serpents, scorpions, vipers . . . ,"[18] words resembling the pronouncements of Prince Andrew and Dolokhov quoted above.

Hélène incorporates what Tolstoy most hated and feared in women: the combined power of beauty and sensual corruption. Her body seems covered by a veneer from all the glances that have passed over it (5:212), he writes, clearly implying that it has thus been greatly cheapened. Her "nakedness" is a dangerous weapon for evil: in the opening salon scene her "full shoulders, bosom and back" are "very much exposed," and Pierre looks at her "with almost frightened, rapturous eyes." In the novel *Resurrection,* the hero sees a shapely streetwalker who is quietly confident of her "vile power" (13:312). In "D'iavol" ("The Devil"), a married man is so tortured by desire for his former mistress that he commits suicide—or, in an alternate ending, kills the mistress. The hero of "Otets Sergii" ("Father Sergius"), in a feverish state, chops off one of his fingers in order to resist a woman who is trying to seduce him. At first Father Sergius suspects that "the devil has assumed a woman's form," as he has "read in the *Lives of the Saints"* (12:358). Then, as she undresses in the next room, "he heard everything. He heard the silk fabric rustling as she took off her dress, how she stepped on the floor with her bare feet; he heard her rubbing her legs with her hand." In *War and Peace,* as Pierre decides that Hélène is destined to be his wife, "he was conscious of the warmth of her body, the fragrance of perfume, and the creaking of her corset when she breathed . . . he saw and sensed the entire charm of her body, which was covered only by her garments" (4:260). At this point, Tolstoy says, she has "power over him already."

Princess Mary is in some ways Hélène's exact opposite. She is thrice removed from the prospect of causing or succumbing to moral corruption—by her life in the country, by her plainness, and by her spirituality. Her somber life consists of duties, prayer, and surreptitious communication with wandering pilgrims. She considers her longings for earthly love an inspiration of the devil (4:279). Conscious that she has suppressed her personal dreams, she achieves a sort of peace until fate intervenes in the person of Nicholas. The development of their relationship allows the fruit of her virtuous life, her inner beauty, to radiate from within her: "All her struggles to improve her inner being, her sufferings, her striving for goodness, her submissiveness, love, self-sacrifice—all this now shone in those radiant eyes, in her delicate smile, and in every trait of her gentle face" (7:28). She becomes an ideal Tolstoyan woman—not only a devoted wife and mother, but an inspiration to her mate and the embodiment of high spirituality. She achieves greater happiness than she had thought possible, yet senses that there is "another sort of happiness, unattainable in this life" (7:277).

Other Fictional Characters

Nicholas Rostov, modeled upon Tolstoy's father, also exhibits several of the author's own traits: "his strength and health, his pagan love of nature, his exaggerated sense of honor and his passion for hunting,"[19] as Henri Troyat writes. Yet as Dmitry Pisarev commented in 1868, Nicholas tends to prefer "not to think," to escape from serious problems by ordering a second bottle of wine.[20] Compared with Prince Andrew and Pierre, who engage in a more deeply Tolstoyan quest for truth, Nicholas seems less concerned by the question of how we should live. He is also more limited in his options, restricted by his early promise to Sonya and subsequently by his own and his father's financial losses.

Nicholas's inability to aid Alexander at Austerlitz immediately precedes and pointedly parallels Andrew's disenchantment with Napoleon. Tolstoy carefully prepares us for both episodes by stressing Andrew's admiration for Napoleon in a conversation he has with his father at Bald Hills, and by emphasizing Nicholas's fervent admiration of the emperor as he reviews Kutuzov's army. Three days later, he even has the Tolstoyan feeling that the emperor can discern what is occurring inside his, Nicholas's, own soul (4:321). After this, though, the two admired figures are rather didactically shown to have feet of clay. Nicholas sees the emperor alone and despondent; Andrew, wounded but inspired by the lofty sky of Austerlitz, hears the words of "his hero" Napoleon "as he might have heard the buzzing of a fly" (4:367). There is an important difference, however. Whereas Andrew seems to gain strength and serenity from the incident, Nicholas's "despair" at having failed to aid Alexander is "all the greater as he felt that his own weakness was the cause of his grief" (4:363).

Whereas Andrew gains spiritual inspiration from the sky, Nicholas is moved, in a similar moment of heightened consciousness, to love life more keenly but also to fear death. As he gazes at the waters of the Danube and the gloriously beautiful sky, Nicholas feels that death is both "above" and "around" him (4:187–88). Much later, when he captures a young, blue-eyed French soldier almost by accident, Nicholas learns that he has earned the St. George Cross. "So others are even more afraid than I am!" he realizes in amazement (6:71).

Nicholas, though good, is rather weak; Dolokhov is not a good man but a strong one. The climactic encounter in which Dolokhov assertively wins 43,000 roubles from Nicholas points up this symmetry. Dolokhov coldly and deliberately sets his goal at 43,000 because his and Sonya's ages total 43, and she has refused him because of Nicholas. After Nicholas's enormous loss, it becomes less likely that he will marry Sonya, who has no fortune of her own.

Dolokhov, a dashing but faintly sinister figure, causes considerable harm to others throughout the novel, seemingly almost without trying. His feat of draining a bottle of rum in the window inspires Pierre, who has been drinking heavily, to insist upon similarly risking death. Much later Dolokhov's daring quite literally inspires Petya Rostov to his death. And the fact that Petya is moved to kiss Dolokhov just before this may remind the reader that Dolokhov had vowed the very deepest friendship to Nicholas not long before depriving him of 43,000 roubles.

Dolokhov indirectly brings both Pierre and Natasha close to death. As he goads Pierre into challenging him to a duel, his mocking smile seems to say: "Ah, this is what I like!" (5:27). Later on, Dolokhov apparently also takes pleasure in masterminding Anatole's furtive wooing and attempted abduction of Natasha, which leads to her near ruin and attempted suicide. The love letter which he composes for Anatole is so well done that Natasha, reading it "for the twentieth time," thinks: "Yes, yes, I love him!" (5:357).

Dolokhov is a complex figure: his code of behavior, which seems to allow such dangerous sport, also requires honor of him. For example, after he is wounded in the duel with Pierre he bursts into tears because his "adored angel mother" may not survive the shock, and he later begs Pierre's forgiveness, declaring that he is glad of the opportunity to do so. These incidents complicate Dolokhov's character and obscure his sinister role in the novel.

Bazdeev and Platon Karataev represent two symmetrically positive forces. However, the influence of Bazdeev is comparatively superficial and temporary, whereas Platon's is more permanent and profound. Pierre meets them at two of the lowest points in his life; after his painful confrontation with Hélène and after he has watched in horror as the French execute prisoners. Each time, Pierre is struggling in despair with questions about the meaning of life and death. Bazdeev treats him paternally; Platon, maternally. Thus Bazdeev repeatedly accompanies his observations with a "gentle, fatherly" smile, and Pierre is several times likened to a child (5:73–77). Platon comforts Pierre "with the gentle singsong caressing tones that old Russian peasant women use," and is "sad that Pierre has no parents, especially a mother." There is no one "dearer than your own mother!" he says, and soon he sings in a "gentle, almost feminine" way (7:51–55). Pierre involuntarily submits to the comforting voices of Bazdeev and Karataev, both of whom suggest that God's great plan is beyond our understanding.

Bazdeev persuades Pierre to become a Freemason, after which he earnestly urges his new beliefs upon Andrew in their conversation at the ferry. Andrew realizes, however, that although Pierre's concern is heartfelt his ideas have little practical wisdom. His initiation into the Society of Freemasons, moreover, is described in a tolerant but parodic manner. Tolstoy himself considered Freemasonry (a secret, philanthropical, and somewhat mystical movement that existed in Russia from the mid-eighteenth century until its suppression under Nicholas I) admirable enough in its aims but rather ridiculous in action.

The peasant Platon Karataev's first name is the Russian form of Plato, and it is tempting to associate him with the peasant Platon from whom the Tolstoyan figure Levin (in *Anna Karenina*) derives spiritual inspiration. Pierre finds comfort in Platon's "roundness," and he relates to Pierre one of Tolstoy's favorite stories, "God Sees the Truth But Speaks Not Soon." In this tale a merchant undergoes brutal torture and ten years of hard labor in Siberia for a murder he did not commit. When the man who had framed him confesses, the merchant responds: "God will forgive you. We are all sinners before God. I suffer for my own sins." When a pardon and compensation finally arrive from the tsar, we are told that God had already forgiven the merchant: he had died. It was not "the story itself," writes Tolstoy, but its "mysterious meaning" and the "rapturous joy" on Platon's face as he told it that joyfully suffused Pierre's soul (7:166–67). This statement becomes somewhat clearer if one recalls that Platon is described as "unable to understand the meaning of words apart from their context." His life, as he saw it, "had meaning only as a particle of a whole that he continually sensed" (7:56). Just as the merchant in Platon's story is "forgiven" by his return to the source of divine love, so Platon naturally feels that his own life is a particle of that source, as Pierre himself realizes at Platon Karataev's death. Pierre's visionlike dream of the "globe of drops" encapsulates this understanding: "In the center is

God, and each drop tries to expand in order to reflect Him as widely as possible. It grows, merges, shrinks, is destroyed on the surface, sinks to the depths, and again floats forth. Here now it is Karataev who has spread out and disappeared" (7:170). Like Platon himself, Pierre intuitively grasps a concept that Prince Andrew had articulated, on his deathbed, but in a form Tolstoy had declared "only thoughts."

Two critics have persuasively related Pierre's dream of the globe of drops to "the Taoist doctrine that at death one is re-absorbed into the total flow."[21] Pierre's vision of his own immersion in water "so that it closed over his head," they observe, is similarly associated with his realization that Platon has died. In a broader sense, they note, the "round" and "almost feminine" Platon may be likened to sages "in touch with the Tao that is the Mother of all and the stream of history." It may thus accord with Tolstoy's theory of historical causation that our limited "freedom is the ability to become coincident with this sensed flow."[22] Natasha, Pierre, and Kutuzov sense a current in their lives and flow with it; Prince Andrew resists; while Napoleon—in Tolstoy's version of history—blindly bucks the tide.

Napoleon and Tolstoyan Determinism

When Tolstoy wrote *War and Peace,* he had long been convinced that historians distort historical truth. The distortion, he believed, was most evident in treatments of famous people thought to have shaped the course of history. Characteristically pushing his view to extremes, Tolstoy decided that so-called great people actually have very little influence on historical events: "A tsar," he insisted in *War and Peace,* "is the slave of history" (6:10). At another point he likens Napoleon to a carved figure on the bow of a ship, which, savages think, powers and directs the vessel—and to a child who, grasping the ribbons and braid that decorate the inside of a carriage, thinks he is driving it (7:100).

These and similar extreme views are clustered in the second epilogue of the novel, where Tolstoy discusses "the will of historical persons" (7:335). He argues that such persons, as well as the orders they give, depend on historical events rather than vice versa. An event will not take place, Tolstoy explains, no matter how many orders are given, without the existence of other causes; when an event does occur, we are too ready to seek out individuals whose orders seem in retrospect to have caused it. As Frank Seeley has observed, such reasoning blurs the

distinction between "cause" in the sense of "sufficient condition" and
"cause" in the sense of "necessary condition."[23] Tolstoy, however, was
intent upon drawing another distinction: "Morally, the cause of an
event appears to be those in power; physically, it is those who submit
to the power" (/:336). He stubbornly adheres to this position throughout the novel. The military campaign of 1812, he claimed, appeared
to depend upon "the will of Napoleon and Alexander," but in order for
their will to be carried out "it was necessary that millions of men, in
whose hands was the real force, the soldiers who fired or transported
provisions and cannons—it was necessary that they consent to carry out
the will of these weak [sic] individuals and that they be led to do so by
an innumerable quantity of complex, diverse causes" (6:9–10). Or,
more simply put, "at the battle of Borodino Napoleon did not shoot
at anyone or kill anyone. All that was done by the soldiers. Thus it
was not he who killed people" (6:230).

The evacuation and burning of Moscow (instead of its ceremonious
surrender to the French) understandably evokes an emotional reaction
from most Russians. In Pushkin's famous phrase, Moscow prepared
"not revelry, not a welcoming gift" but "a conflagration for the impatient hero."[24] Tolstoy himself carefully anticipates this moment by describing Napoleon as self-centered and supremely confident of his own
power: "Everything outside of him," Tolstoy writes, "had no meaning
for him because everything in the world, it seemed to him, depended
entirely on his will" (6:27). Then, as Napoleon is about to occupy
Moscow, Tolstoy takes evident pleasure in having him dream of being
magnanimous to its humble citizens as they surrender. As Tolstoy explains, the French generals faced a twofold problem: how to tell Napoleon the terrible news that the Russians would not surrender, but,
still worse, how to keep him from appearing ridiculous (6:339). When
the French army finally abandons Moscow and retreats in disarray, Tolstoy compares its movements to the reflexive spasms of a mortally
wounded animal. It is then that he likens Napoleon to a child who,
while playing with the decorations inside a carriage, is convinced that
he is driving it.

Tolstoy calls the evacuation and burning of Moscow "just as inevitable as the retreat of the army without fighting beyond Moscow after
the battle of Borodino" (6:288). "Every Russian," he adds, "could have
predicted what happened, not by reasoning but by a feeling inside of
us and in each of our fathers." In an unpublished foreword to the first
chapters of *War and Peace,* Tolstoy expressed the secret hope that Rus-

sia's triumph of 1812 "was not accidental, but lay in the essence of the character of the Russian people and army."[25] Of the one-eyed Kutuzov—who is often called "blind" in the novel but whose patient strategy crucially contributes to Russia's triumph—Tolstoy writes: "For the representative of the Russian people—after the enemy had been destroyed and Russia had been placed on the pinnacle of her glory—for this Russian there was nothing left to do as a Russian. For the representative of the people's war, nothing remained except death. And he died" (7:215). The facts do not support the contrast between Tolstoy's Kutuzov, a simple, unaffected, wise Russian general who passively submits to events, and his Napoleon, a stupid, arrogant French poseur who believes he can impose his will on history.[26] However, this contrast illustrates Tolstoy's views on the role of so-called great men in history, as well as his aggressively elaborated theory of determinism.

This theory is painstakingly developed in the second epilogue. Our actions, Tolstoy contends, are far less free than we suppose. A person who commits a criminal act, he explains, may have been driven to do so for a variety of reasons (7:342). If, Tolstoy insists, we could understand the almost infinite chain of causes and circumstances leading up to and attending a particular action, it would be clear that the action was inevitable. As an illustration, he analyzes the simple action of moving one's arm (7:347). Free as the action may seem, he argues, it is necessarily limited in three respects. First, there are physical limitations—the structure of one's arm and any obstacles in its path. Second, the action is temporally limited: in retrospect, Tolstoy claims, we realize that no different action could have occurred at that exact same instant. (Even though the action seems free as we perform it, he suggests, it later appears less so in proportion to the time that has elapsed since then and the consequences stemming from it.) Finally, Tolstoy reasons, we are limited by causes (even the desire to perform an action without a cause is itself a cause). He therefore declares: "In order to imagine a perfectly free person, one not subject to the law of necessity, we must imagine him alone, *outside of space, outside of time,* and *outside of dependence upon causes.*"

Tolstoy then differentiates between reason, which expresses the laws of necessity (though they in their totality are beyond our comprehension) and conscious awareness, which expresses what we perceive as the freedom of our actions (7:350). In his opinion, our consciousness "tells" us that we are not outside of space but are outside of time and outside of causes, since we "feel" that we ourselves are the cause of every manifestation of our lives. That which we term free will, he concludes, is actually a natural, predictable force, like electricity or gravity; it is similarly subject to laws, but in this case laws that we fail to discern. Just as we have had to admit that, despite appearances, the other planets do not orbit the earth, so "we must renounce our non-existent freedom and acknowledge a dependence that we do not perceive" (7:355).

Though one can disagree with some of Tolstoy's arguments, especially those on temporal limitation, it is virtually impossible to disprove his conclusion, with its self-substantiating emphasis upon the limited, illusory nature of human consciousness. A vastly superior, "infinite" consciousness, capable of perceiving literally all circumstances leading up to and surrounding an action, could perhaps indeed see the action as predictable, even inevitable.

The creator of a literary work may be said to have a godlike perspective on the destinies of his characters. Of course, the author also controls these destinies—as invisibly or visibly as his intentions and abilities permit. Throughout *War and Peace*, Tolstoy adheres to his theory of determinism as convincingly and artistically as possible: he depicts both historical and fictional events as apparently inevitable while preserving for his characters their illusion of free will. The novel opens with the suggestion that Napoleon is the "Antichrist"; within a few pages Lise asks Pierre, who is discussing Napoleon, if he believes that assassination shows greatness of soul. All of this ironically anticipates Pierre's subsequent conviction that he is predestined to assassinate Napoleon, who, he has decided, is the Antichrist. Still later, however, Tolstoy suggests that Pierre was "destined" *not* to kill Napoleon (6:403).

Other events are explicitly described as inevitable—the duel between Pierre and Dolokhov begins, for example: "It was evident that the affair so lightly begun could already not be prevented but was taking its own course independent of the will of men and had to happen" (5:30).

Similar views permeate what one critic has termed "the novel's crucial scene."[27] Captured in Moscow by the French, Pierre watches them execute prisoners in the belief that he too will be shot: "He had only one wish—that the frightful thing that had to happen should happen quickly" (7:45). The French soldiers do in fact hurry, "as if to finish an essential but unpleasant and incomprehensible task." Having decided to shoot the prisoners in pairs, bound to a post, they begin. Pierre turns away, but upon hearing sounds "louder than the most terrible thunder claps," he looks around to see smoke and soldiers with pale faces doing "something" beside a nearby pit.

They position the next pair. "Pierre again did not want to look and turned away; but again a horrible explosion struck his ears." Again he sees smoke and soldiers with pale, frightened faces doing "something" near the post. He also notices that all those present, even the French, seem to experience the very same horror as he. "But who is really doing this?" he wonders. "They are all suffering just the same as I. Who, then? Who?"

Next a young factory worker is led to the post alone; Pierre, the sixth, is spared in order to witness the final execution, although he fails to realize this. No longer able to turn away, he cannot "take his eyes off" the young victim: "A command must have been heard; after the command, the shots of eight rifles must have resounded. But Pierre, much as he later tried to remember, did not hear the slightest sound of the shots." This third execution resembles in its numbing horror a silent film strip. During the first two, Pierre could not look but was shocked by the sound of the shooting. This time, however, he watches in frozen silence: "He only saw the factory worker for some reason suddenly sinking down upon the ropes." Here Tolstoy characteristically employs the technique of "making strange": for a brief but vivid moment, we wonder why, "for some reason," the young worker's body sinks down upon the ropes that bind him. Once again Pierre sees soldiers with pale, frightened faces doing "something"—this time next to the factory worker, and the reader again envisions soldiers moving the dead from post to pit. Even the smoke functions similarly, as one pictures what created it. Of course, this entire episode is also "made strange" by the fact that Pierre has never before witnessed such horrors, which seem the more terrible for their apparent inevitability. A grim note of inevitability also echoes in the memories that haunt him later: "Whenever he closed his eyes, he would see before him the factory worker's face, especially dreadful in its simplicity, and, in their agitation, the still more dreadful faces of the involuntary murderers" (7:50).

A revealing comparison between the artistic techniques and moral and philosophical concerns of Tolstoy and Dostoevsky may be obtained by juxtaposing this scene with the observations on executions made by Prince Myshkin in *Idiot* (*The Idiot*). (Whereas Dostoevsky, like Tolstoy's Pierre, had fully expected to be executed himself on one occasion, Tolstoy had been horrified, like Dostoevsky's Myshkin, by a guillotining he had witnessed in France.) Myshkin says he was particularly shocked that the victim, a strong, brave man, "cried, white as paper."[28] What causes a man "who has never cried," he wonders, to cry from fright? "What happens at that minute to the soul, what causes it such convulsions?" It is "an outrage to the soul," Myshkin concludes, to kill a person because he has killed. "I saw this a month ago, and it is still before my eyes. About five times I've dreamed of it."

Like Pierre, Myshkin is haunted by visions of the execution, but in his case they have also been internalized as dreams. A similar but more basic difference is that whereas Pierre watches in frozen horror, Myshkin probes the victim's inner experience. Even the "pale, frightened" faces of Tolstoy's executioner-soldiers are transferred in Dostoevsky to the victim ("white as paper"). Still more important, Pierre's question "Who is doing this?" is formulated by Myshkin as "How can one person do this to another?" And this leads to the crucial comparison. Whereas Dostoevsky characteristically arraigns a world in which such atrocities can exist, Tolstoy sees them, in *War and Peace,* as grimly inevitable: beyond our control ("the frightful thing that had to happen"), beyond our comprehension ("an essential but unpleasant and incomprehensible task"), and even beyond our direct responsibility ("the involuntary murderers").

Chapter Five
Anna Karenina

The first extant reference to Tolstoy's most artistically satisfying novel is found in his wife's diary for February 1870. His intention, she wrote there, was to depict an adulterous woman of high society as "not guilty but merely pitiful."[1] Tolstoy began the novel only in March of 1873, inspired by the opening of a fragmentary tale by Pushkin. "That's the way for us to write," he said: The author "jumps into the action at once." Tolstoy profited from Pushkin's example: the dynamic, tightly constructed beginning of *Anna Karenina* is exemplary among nineteenth-century novels. It began appearing serially in 1875 in Katkov's *Russian Messenger,* although the eighth and last part, which expressed unpatriotic ideas about the Russo-Turkish War of 1878–79, had to be published separately. The novel enjoyed a glorious success among both readers and critics, although Tolstoy himself never liked it.

In addition to Pushkin, literary sources for *Anna Karenina* include George Eliot's *Adam Bede*[2] and Alexandre Dumas's *L'Homme-femme.* In Boris Eikhenbaum's view, the novel's epigraph ("Vengeance is mine; I will repay") suggests an answer to Dumas's thesis that a woman should be killed if she is unfaithful to her husband and deserts him and her children: such a woman need not be killed, for she will perish at God's hand.[3] Tolstoy's selection of the epigraph was influenced by his reading of Arthur Schopenhauer.

As in *War and Peace,* many of this novel's characters are derived from life. Anna's fate parallels that of Anna Pirogova, the mistress of Tolstoy's neighbor A. N. Biblikov, who threw herself under a train in 1872. Konstantin Levin is modeled upon the author himself, and his last name is based on Tolstoy's first name, Lev. Nicholas Levin is patterned on Tolstoy's brother Dmitry, who also lived with a former prostitute named Masha and also died of tuberculosis.

Tolstoy wrote *Anna Karenina* during a difficult period in his life, and his letters reveal that he struggled long and painfully to complete it: "I want to give it up, I dislike it so much," he wrote to Countess Alexandra Tolstaya in 1874.[4] Tolstoy came to view adultery as a cheap and easy topic that could not have a positive influence upon his readers.

In draft form, the novel began with Anna's affair already in progress, and she was provocatively pictured (like Hélène in the opening of *War and Peace*) at a soiree in a low-cut dress. In subsequent versions, however, she gradually ceased to be vulgar, stout, and unattractive and became lovely, graceful, and charming. Karenin and Vronsky, on the other hand, evolved into less positive characters.[5] Levin and Kitty were not present in the earliest drafts; but when they did appear the title was, for a while, *Two Marriages*.

Structure and Symmetry

Commentators have frequently disagreed about the unity of *Anna Karenina*. The drama involving Anna, Karenin, and Vronsky seems to form the main plot, and yet the story of Levin and Kitty prominently rivals it. Some critics have even complained that the sharply contrasting love relationships vie too obviously for the reader's attention. Sergey Rachinsky wrote to Tolstoy that his novel had "no architecture," suggesting that two themes are developed side by side—magnificently, but disconnectedly. Tolstoy replied that he was "proud" of the novel's architecture: he had constructed its arches carefully so that the keystone would remain invisible. "The structural link," he declared, is an "inner" one—"Not the plot or the relationships (friendships) between the characters."[6] Tolstoy did not explain just what this "link" was. He had written to Nikolay Strakhov in April of 1876: "if I were to try to say in words everything that I intended to express in my novel, I would have to write the same novel I wrote from the beginning."[7]

Some critics have proposed the Stiva-Dolly story as a third plot line, and it is also important, from the very beginning, as a "family" situation. But Sydney Schultze has shown that the novel can be grouped into thirty-four segments, alternately devoted to Anna and Levin, its principal structural strands.[8] More generally, the main focus shifts quite regularly from Levin to Anna. In Part I, for example, wc first follow Levin's arrival in Moscow and its consequences, then Anna's. This process culminates when Levin actually goes to meet Anna in Part VII. (Exceptions are Part II, emphasizing Anna, and Part VIII, emphasizing Levin.)

Anna comes to Moscow to repair her brother Stiva's marriage; Levin, to propose to Kitty. Critics have frequently noted the irony in the fact that in seeking to save a marriage, Anna is attracted to Vronsky at the station and eventually destroys her own. As Schultze has noted, the novel falls neatly into two halves, with the twin "marriages" of Anna and Levin as the transition between them: Anna and Vronsky begin living as a couple at the end of Part IV; Levin's marriage to Kitty opens Part V. Moreover, the Anna and Levin plots are bound together by common themes, so that the novel's eight parts could be entitled Upsets, Reorientation, Plans, Couples, Early Married Life, Country Life, Consequences, and The Future.[9]

In her book *The Architecture of "Anna Karenina,"* Elisabeth Stenbock-Fermor argues that the Oblonsky party, at which Kitty accepts Levin's marriage proposal, is the novel's "keystone," flanked on each side by four symmetrical pillars. One and eight are the "family idea," two and seven involve a search for the "meaning of life," and the other four are all railroad scenes: Vronsky meets Anna, Vronsky and Anna, Anna's death, Vronsky remembers Anna.[10]

Anna Karenina begins by differentiating between happy and unhappy families, a comment that anticipates the contrast between Levin's marriage and Anna's. The Oblonskys, at the center of attention in the beginning, are symmetrically related to these two marriages: Stiva Oblonsky is Anna's brother, and Dolly Oblonskaya's sister Kitty marries Levin. This symmetry also affects the novel's structure. Stiva's affair with a French governess is followed by his sister Anna's affair with Vronsky; Dolly's painful disappointment in Stiva is followed by her sister Kitty's painful disappointment in Vronsky. In short, Vronsky figures in two triangles with blood relationships to the Oblonskys:

Opening Focus

VRONSKY	↓	VRONSKY
↑		↑
KARENIN–ANNA ——	STIVA–DOLLY ——	KITTY–LEVIN
(sister/brother)	*(sisters)*	

Also structurally, Vronsky's early emotional exploitation of Kitty is balanced much later by Anna's treatment of Levin. And the latter, combined with Lidia Ivanovna's manipulation of Karenin, makes faintly traced but unrealized squares out of the two triangles. As in *War and Peace,* family resemblances extend to characteristic details. Stiva, found out in his affair with the governess, thinks "it's my fault, but I'm not guilty." Anna, after enticing Vronsky away from Kitty at the ball, remarks: "I'm not guilty, or only guilty a very little" (8:112). "Oh, how like Stiva you said that!" Dolly exclaims.

Numerous other episodes occur in pairs. Levin twice proposes marriage to Kitty after he is twice unable to reveal (to Stiva and to Koznyshev) his intention to do so. Karenin is twice called "a saint," by Anna and by Lidia Ivanovna. Anna's death is prefigured by two others: a watchman's and a horse's. Moreover, both she and Vronsky have approximately the same ominous dream of a peasant beating on iron that foreshadows her death: *railroad* is "iron road" in Russian.

Anna suggests that she is made up of two separate people, and at the same time observes how curious it is that her husband and lover are both named Alexey. Structurally, her dream of both "Alexeys" simultaneously becoming "her husbands" as Karenin weeps and exclaims "How good it is now!" (8:168), anticipates the scene when both Alexeys appear at her bedside and Karenin sobs like a child, overcome with joyous love and forgiveness for Anna and Vronsky (8:453). At this point Vronsky feels that he and Karenin have "suddenly exchanged roles."

Karenin is twice likened to a man who has had an aching tooth removed when he learns that his painful suspicion is correct, that Anna loves Vronsky. After Anna's death, Vronsky is repeatedly said to suffer from a toothache: the image has been realized.[11] And just as Anna's death is associated with her lover Alexey's real toothache, so her husband Alexey's metaphorical toothache is linked to the "death" of their marriage.

Though Stiva and Dolly do not constitute a major plot line, they have important roles to play throughout the novel. Dolly is a force promoting family unity. Not only does she forgive Stiva and hold her own marriage together; as a Tolstoyan unlikely prophet, she correctly foresees marriages that many consider unlikely, including the union of Kitty and Levin (8:47). Later, Dolly emphatically urges Karenin to stay married to Anna ("Anything but a divorce!"), adding that she has "forgiven" and he must do so as well (8:433). Affable though he is, Stiva causes considerable harm.[12] Though his asking Anna to Moscow results in solace for Dolly, it is also the first fateful step leading to Anna's disastrous affair. Again unwittingly, Stiva causes double discord between Kitty and Levin: by bringing Vasenka Veslovsky to visit them (whereupon Levin becomes viciously jealous); and by taking Levin to see Anna (whereupon Kitty becomes just as jealous, evidently recalling Anna's capture of Vronsky). And, of course, there is also Stiva's own family-disrupting affair. Speaking of *War and Peace,* John Bayley has suggested that "in a sense Tolstoy's most damning comment on the nature of war" is "that Dolokhov gets on so well at it."[13] The same could be said of Russian society as shown in *Anna Karenina:* Stiva Oblonsky moves too easily within it.

Anna's "Guilt"

The epigraph to *Anna Karenina* comes from the Bible: "Vengeance is mine; I will repay" (followed by "saith the Lord," Rom. 12:19). Its significance for the novel has long been a subject of controversy. Boris Eikhenbaum has collected various opinions, from Dostoevsky's view that only God fully understands human criminality to Mark Aldanov's insinuation that the "enigmatic" epigraph masks the author's inability to give a moral meaning to his work: "As long as the Oblonskys and Tverskayas live in clover, it is difficult to conceive the death of Anna as an act of higher justice." To Mikhail Gromeka's opinion that to wreck a marriage, the only true basis for love and family happiness, is to invite destruction, Eikhenbaum responds that he "completely ignores the tragic, the inescapable in Anna's fate, which compels the reader to pardon her and to be puzzled by the epigraph." He also quotes V. Veresaev's opinion of 1907 that "vital life" cannot "tolerate" a woman's being merely a mother or merely a mistress (as he saw Anna's roles with Karenin and Vronsky, respectively), along with Tolstoy's reaction in his old age, that this was "clever," but that he had chosen the epigraph "simply to convey the idea that the evil [*durnoe*] that man does has as its consequence only bitterness, which comes not from man, but from God, and which Anna Karenina, too, experienced." Finally, Eikhenbaum develops his own interpretation: "the inescapable consequences of 'evil' are, not vengeance by man, but his own suffering, which 'does not come from man.'"[14]

Vladimir Nabokov views the "implications" of the epigraph as follows: "First, Society had no right to judge Anna; second, Anna had no right to punish Vronski by her revengeful suicide." In Nabokov's opinion, the "moral" of the novel "is certainly not that having committed adultery, Anna had to pay for it . . . had Anna remained with Karenin and skillfully concealed from the world her affair, she would not have paid for it first with her happiness and then with her life." The "real moral point," he adds, is this: "Love cannot be exclusively carnal because then it is egotistic, and being egotistic it destroys instead of creating. It is thus sinful."[15] Nabokov also persuasively argues that the novel be titled *Anna Karenin* in English.[16] However, there is no ideal solution to the problem of Anna's surname: when Vronsky thinks about "where he can meet *Karenina*" at the end of Part I, the effect is quite untranslatable into English. The name *Karenin* itself is based upon the Greek *karenon* ("reason, head, intellect"), in a subtle reinforcement of Karenin's judgmental attitude toward Anna, and of his coldly rational approach to life. The distinction between head and heart is perhaps as central to *Anna Karenina* as it is to *War and Peace*.

At the railroad station, Anna's attraction to Vronsky is revealed by a "gleam" in her eyes that she repeatedly fails to "extinguish" (8:72), and this same "joyous gleam" flares up in her eyes when Vronsky speaks with her at the ball. Kitty is then astonished to see Vronsky's expression of "submission and fear," recalling the look of an intelligent, guilty dog. She is also aghast upon detecting "something horrible and cruel in Anna's charm," something "strange, satanic and enchanting" (8:93–96). Soon afterward Anna leaves the ball without staying for supper, but her apparent efforts not to arouse Vronsky's passion have failed. The word *satanic* (*besovskii*) is a vestige of earlier versions in which Anna was repeatedly seen as devillike.[17]

After the ball the Oblonsky children quickly notice a change in their aunt. When Anna first arrived in Moscow, they had been warmly affectionate, but now, Tolstoy tells us, they "ceased to love her"—perhaps because children "are sensitive, and they felt that Anna was now entirely different from the person they had liked so much" (8:111). This strikes a subtly ominous note: Anna's passion already tends to exclude other people, and the children apparently sense this. In 1865, Tolstoy had written to the Countess Alexandra: "you can't deceive children—they are wiser than we are."[18] Later in the novel, the Oblonsky children are drawn to Levin because, Tolstoy suggests, "there was not a sign of dissembling in him." Dissembling, he adds, may deceive the most intelligent adult but not "the most limited child" (8:295).

When Anna returns to St. Petersburg, the first face she notices is her husband's: "'Oh, my God! What has happened to his ears?' she thought, gazing at his cold, imposing figure and especially at the gristly ears that so struck her now, propping up the rim of his round hat" (8:118). This brief passage illustrates three favorite Tolstoyan narrative techniques: inner monologue, body language, and making strange. The change in Anna is masterfully reflected in her feeling that Karenin has changed for the worse, which has been aptly likened to "Emma

Bovary's discovery that Charles makes uncouth noises while eating."[19] When Anna arrives home, she is similarly disappointed by her beloved son, Seryozha, and friend Lidia Ivanovna, both of whom suddenly seem less attractive than before. This anticipates her frame of mind before she commits suicide, when everyone around her seems grotesque and ugly. In sharp contrast, Levin feels blissfully in tune with his surroundings after Kitty accepts his proposal. Whereas their love relationship promotes harmony, Tolstoy implies, guilty passion separates people one from another.

Anna soon tells Vronsky, who has followed her to St. Petersburg, that he makes her "feel guilty of something" (8:156). She asks him to return to Moscow and seek Kitty's forgiveness. "You don't want that," he replies, adding that she is his "entire life" and wondering if "happiness" is possible: "She strained all the forces of her mind to say what she ought; but instead she fixed on him a look filled with love and did not answer anything." Vronsky correctly interprets this eloquent look as a confession of love. Even though Anna keeps on trying to dissuade him, "her look said something entirely different."

Karenin adopts a rather conventional approach toward the problem of his wife's guilt. When he suspects Anna's true feelings for Vronsky, he decides to warn her on four counts: first, the opinion of society; second, the religious meaning of marriage; third, the consequences for their son; fourth, her own unhappiness. The fact that Karenin places social propriety first suggests the rigidity of his attitude toward Anna's "guilt," as does the fact that he punctuates the elaboration of his plan by cracking the joints of his fingers (8:161–62). But when he does warn her, Karenin stresses the second point: "Our lives are bound together not by people, but by God. Only a crime can break this bond, and that kind of crime brings a strong punishment" (8:164).

Three pages later, Karenin's idea of crime becomes almost terrifyingly graphic. When Anna first yields to Vronsky, we are told that Vronsky felt as a murderer must feel upon seeing the body of his victim. "This body, which he had deprived of life, was their love, the first period of their love." We are left with the ominous expectation that punishment must follow.

Karenin's warning that to break God's bond brings punishment echoes the novel's epigraph. Although he prefaces this echo by referring to society's awareness of Anna's attitude, he insists that jealousy is beneath him. This allows Anna to decide that Karenin himself is indifferent to their relationship except as it appears to society. This in turn might seem a convenient rationalization on her part, except that Karenin has been slow to "notice" the change in her not merely out of contempt for jealousy. At first, then, Tolstoy carefully balances the Karenins' attitudes, although critics have objected that we are given insufficient information about why Anna had agreed to a marriage with him to begin with. Karenin himself, we learn only in Part V, had no strong feelings about her, but was pressured into marriage by Anna's aunt.

After her affair with Vronsky begins, Anna exclaims "My God! Forgive me!" Tolstoy, however, adds: "She felt so guilty, so much to blame, that it remained only for her to humble herself and to ask forgiveness; but she had no one in life now except him [Vronsky], so it was to him that she addressed her prayer for forgiveness" (8:167). In severing the bond established by God, Anna has lost the ability to pray meaningfully to Him; she now tells Vronsky: "I have no one except you. Remember that." These words, with their implication of possessiveness and isolation, contain the seeds of her destruction.

There is also a destructive element in Anna's openness. When Vronsky's horse Frou-Frou falls during the race, she displays "unseemly" agitation, and replies to her husband's questions: "I love him, I am his lover, this is unbearable, I am afraid, I hate you. . . . Do with me what you like" (8:236). Unlike some of her friends, Anna is ominously unable to conduct her affair with socially acceptable discretion. Later, when she insists upon going to the theater and thereby challenges society, her openness becomes almost flagrantly self-destructive.

After Anna confesses to Karenin, he tells himself that she is guilty, not he (8:308). His jealousy, Tolstoy tells us, had now yielded to a desire that she be punished for her crime. He therefore decides to act in such a way as to punish her, though he does not admit this to himself. Only by insisting that his wife live as before, without seeing Vronsky, he concludes, will he be acting in conformity with the precepts of his religion (8:311).

Soon afterward, Anna decides that she has tried in vain to love Karenin, and that she is not at fault if God has filled her with a desire to love and to live (8:322). In this particular attempt at self-justification she resembles her brother Stiva, who feels no guilt at all over the fact that he, a handsome, amorous man of thirty-four, is not in love with his wife (8:9).

When Dolly urges Karenin to forgive Anna, he says that he hates her for all the evil she has done to him. "Love those who hate you,"

Dolly replies. "But it is impossible," Karenin objects, "to love those whom you hate" (8:433–34). Dolly's advice to Karenin echoes the words in the Bible following the epigraph (Rom. 12:21): "overcome evil with good." Karenin is now so self-righteous, however, that he cannot accept this. Even at his most noble moment—when Anna fears she is dying in childbirth—this same attitude mars Karenin's magnanimity. "I have seen her and forgiven," he tells Vronsky. "The joy of forgiving has revealed to me my duty. I have forgiven completely. I want to turn the other cheek. I want to give my coat when my cloak is taken. I only pray to God not to deprive me of the joy of forgiving!" (8:454). Despite his apparent sincerity, Karenin's joy is clearly self-centered: he is concerned only with himself, both in giving and in receiving. Later, when Stiva suggests a divorce, Karenin once again derives satisfaction from imagining himself—in accordance with the Sermon on the Mount—turning the other cheek and giving up his coat when his cloak has been taken (8:473). At this point, however, Anna refuses to accept a divorce because it is the product of "*his* generosity." She leaves Seryozha with Karenin and goes abroad with Vronsky, who has declined a desirable post and resigned his commission. The lovers thus abandon much that had previously given their lives meaning.

Society had no code to apply to such a love. Vronsky's mother first considers her son's affair rather stylish, but becomes displeased when it begins to control his life. Vronsky himself is said to be "fortunate" in having formulated a code of conduct for himself (only women may be lied to, only husbands may be deceived, etc.), but he seems less than fortunate when he suddenly realizes that Anna's pregnancy is "not fully defined by his code of rules" (8:337).

Vronsky has often been called a "superfluous man," a term applied to several heroes of nineteenth-century Russian literature who are prevented by their upbringing and by society from realizing their true potential. Such men typically turn—in desperation, but with limited success—to reading, travel, and philanthropy. Tolstoy likens Vronsky, in his seizing upon politics, new books, and paintings, to a hungry animal, seeking food in every object it encounters (9:37). Also, such men typically (as in Turgenev's "Asya" and *Rudin*) disappoint the women they love by their lack of initiative. Thus when Anna tells Vronsky that she has admitted their affair to her husband: "If at this news he would decisively, passionately and without a moment's hesitation say to her 'Give up everything and fly with me!'—she would abandon her son and go away with him. But . . . he only seemed vaguely offended by something" (8:347). Unlike most superfluous men, however, Vronsky does eventually make a commitment to Anna, and he later engages in reasonably successful philanthropic activities.

Not long before Anna's suicide, Tolstoy offers a carefully balanced analysis of her relationship with Vronsky:

The irritation that divided them had no external cause, and all attempted explanations not only failed to remove it but even increased it. It was an internal irritation, based for her on a diminution of his love; for him, on a regret that for her sake he had placed himself in a difficult position which she, instead of trying to alleviate, made still more difficult. Neither one nor the other spoke about the causes of their irritation, but they considered each other in the wrong and under any pretext attempted to prove this to each other (9:332).

The situation is, to be sure, aggravated by society's intolerance of Anna's frank openness regarding her affair. Moreover, communications between Vronsky and Anna are often delayed or misinterpreted, almost as if Fate were taking a hand in the matter.

Lidia Ivanovna, Karenin's friend who swoops in to console him after Anna's infidelity, demonstrates the potential cruelty of pious righteousness. Indeed, her imperious goodness seems calculated to point up Anna's helpless vulnerability. Seizing control of Karenin's household, Lidia tells Seryozha that his father is a saint and that his mother has died (9:88). She then persuades Karenin to refuse Anna's desperate plea to visit Seryozha, explaining that the boy thinks she is dead. Tolstoy takes the irony still further when Lidia writes to Anna that reminding Seryozha of his mother might cause him to ask difficult questions, in a letter that "wounded Anna to the depths of her soul" (9:98).

Seryozha, however, keeps his mother delicately alive in his heart. He refuses to believe in her death, searches for her while out walking, and secretly prays at night for her return. The boy's faith is justified by Anna's surprise visit on his birthday, and their mutual joy is touchingly intensified by the fact that her intrusion must imminently be discovered.

Tolstoy appropriately has Dolly Oblonskaya express two key attitudes on the question of Anna's "guilt." As the novel begins, Anna persuades Dolly to forgive her husband's infidelity, so Dolly's view of Anna's own subsequent infidelity carries special weight. As we have seen, Dolly urges Karenin to forgive Anna, on grounds that one should "love those who hate you." Much later Dolly visits Anna, who asks her opinion "of my position." Dolly replies: "I have no opinion. I have always loved you, and if one loves, one loves the whole person just as he or she is, and not as one would like them to be" (9:198). Anna carefully considers Dolly's answer, and then declares: "If you had any sins, they would all be forgiven you for your coming here and for those words." By drawing upon these views expressed by Dolly to Anna and Karenin, we may isolate two crucial aspects of the novel's epigraph in terms of the Tolstoyan question of how we should live: we should not judge others, and we should forgive others. Nabokov's interpretation that society had no right to judge Anna and that she had no right to punish Vronsky by her suicide is but one of several possible applications of these imperatives within the novel.

Levin and Kitty

By contrast to the progressively more destructive relationship between Anna and Vronsky, there is an increasingly life-affirming quality in the story of Kitty and Levin. Like Pierre and Natasha in *War and Peace*, they are from the beginning associated by suggestions of childhood and fairy tale–like pleasure. At the skating rink, Levin is struck by Kitty's expression "of childish clarity and goodness" and by the "childishness of her face" (8:38). Her smile, we learn, always carried him off to "an enchanted world where he experienced tender, soft feelings like those he recalled from rare days of his early childhood." He also recalls that he used to associate Kitty with an English fairy tale. Early in the novel, Levin himself is compared to a "boy," a "twelve-year-old girl," and a "child" (8:27, 28, 43). As with Natasha and Pierre, these introductory descriptions link Kitty and Levin at a time when marriage still seems quite unlikely: Kitty refuses Levin's first proposal.

Even in this refusal, however, Kitty shows a life-affirming sensitivity to Levin's feelings. Sensing that he is about to propose, she painfully realizes that she must hurt a "very dear" person who loves her. "My God, do I really have to tell him myself?" she wonders (8:57). "I'll go away," she thinks. "I haven't done anything wrong." All this strikingly resembles Natasha's reaction to Denisov's proposal in *War and Peace*. Like Kitty, Natasha feels sorry for the "very dear" person she must offend. "What am I guilty of?" she asks her mother. "Do you

want me to go tell him?" her mother replies with a smile (5:67). When
Kitty rejects Levin's proposal, she looks "straight into his face, as if
imploring him to have mercy." As he musters the courage to propose,
her look remains "imploring and caressing"; after refusing, Kitty pities
Levin "with her entire soul, especially because she herself had caused
him to suffer."

Kitty's keen empathy no doubt helps her to understand Levin's second proposal, when he bashfully writes down only the first letters of
numerous words that she almost miraculously guesses. Her capacity for
pity is no less remarkable. After Levin, grimly convinced that he must
conceal nothing, compels her to read the diary accounts of his impure
past, Kitty gives free vent to her revulsion, but then, "taking pity on
his desperate face," acknowledges that it was all "for the best." Later,
when Kitty's birth pains began, she tells Levin: "Please, don't be
afraid, it's nothing." Still later, when Anna mentions her fondness for
Levin "with obvious ill intent," Kitty (who has been painfully jealous)
looks at her "with sympathy" and decides that she is "terribly pitiable."

After Vronsky turns his attention from Kitty to Anna, Dolly tries
to console Kitty but finds her unreceptive. Then, when Dolly mentions
Levin, Kitty exclaims: "Why bring Levin into this? . . . I will never,
never do what you are doing—return to a man who has betrayed you
and loved another woman" (8:140). Both fall silent for a time, lowering their heads. Dolly is deeply hurt:

But suddenly she heard the rustle of a dress and also the emerging sound of
suppressed sobbing, and someone's arms encircled her neck from below. Kitty
was on her knees before her.
    "Dolly dear, I am so terribly unhappy!" she guiltily whispered. (8:140–41)

Kitty's remorse is doubly touching because Dolly hardly expects such
a sudden transformation and because Tolstoy vividly "makes it strange"
("someone's arms . . . from below"). The sisters then restore their former relationship, and Dolly realizes that Kitty is "ready to love Levin."
Her outburst of hostility is thus a shameful but ultimately positive
stage of personal growth, as is her final realization, at the spa, that in
attempting to help others she must be guided by her own heart rather
than by a set of rules.

Levin must grow still more in terms of the Tolstoyan question of
how we should live. After Kitty refuses his first proposal, his look says:
"I hate everyone, including you and myself." When he hears of Kitty's

illness, he is "pleased that she was suffering, she, who had caused him to suffer so much." After three months of marriage, however, when Kitty angrily reproaches him for arriving home late:

Only then did he clearly understand for the first time what he had not understood when he had led her out of church after the wedding. He understood that not only was she close to him, but that now he did not know where she ended and he began. . . . For the first minute he was offended, but at the same instant he felt that he could not be offended by her, that she was he himself. (9:55–56)

This understanding develops in Levin still more near the end of the novel, when Kitty and their baby Mitya escapes from a dangerous thunderstorm and he realizes how much he loves his son.

Unlike Levin, Kitty has or acquires the spontaneous ability to help others in distress that sets Natasha and Pierre apart from the other characters in *War and Peace*. Inspired by her friend Varenka at the spa, Kitty decides "to forget herself and to love others" (8:248). She is especially "enticed" by the idea of reading the Gospel to the sick, criminals, and the dying. Though her good intentions may seem naive and even slightly dramatic, they are free from affectation and self-involvement. In this respect her aim resembles Pierre's "modest" attempt to live for others, as he describes it to Andrew in *War and Peace*. After Kitty's failure to help the Petrovs, she retains what she has learned yet "awakens" fully to the dangers of "posing and boastfulness" (8:261).

All this serves as an important prelude to Kitty's relationship with Levin's brother Nicholas. Since Nicholas is living with a former prostitute, Levin endeavors to prevent Kitty from accompanying him to visit his dying brother, yet she helps Nicholas whereas Levin irritates him. After finally persuading her husband to let her see Nicholas, Kitty begins to talk to him "with that sympathetic, quiet animation which does not offend and which is characteristic only of women" (9:68). By contrast, Levin keeps thinking morosely that death is imminent, and his brother painfully senses this. Kitty, however, feels a natural pity for the dying man: "in her woman's soul, pity did not produce the feeling of horror and disgust that it did in her husband, but rather a need to act, to find out all the details of his condition and to help him." In this instance, Tolstoy twice seems to suggest that the quality of spontaneous altruism is a particularly female virtue. Thanks to Kitty's quiet, efficient efforts, Nicholas soon has "a new look of hope."

Whereas Kitty realizes quite early in the novel that she must live by her heart rather than by rules, Levin continually attempts to reason his way toward truth, and his personal growth is also comparatively self-centered. Even his admirable understanding that by hurting Kitty he is only hurting himself leads him to conclude that "to prove her wrong would mean to irritate her still more" and widen the rift between them. Earlier, while mowing with the peasants, he derives "particular pleasure" from the fact that he does not lag behind them (8:277). And the "questions of life and death" that nearly drive him to suicide near the end of the novel are essentially solipsistic. (For example, "If I don't accept the answers given by Christianity to the questions of my life, then what answers do I accept?") What upsets him most, we are told, is that other people do not share his frenzied anxiety about such questions: "Are these people sincere?" he wonders (9:384). Levin is evidently closer to the mark when he finally concludes that true knowledge is beyond reason (9:393), a conclusion that follows and pointedly counters the statement Anna hears just before she commits suicide: "Reason is given to man to enable him to escape his troubles" (9:362).

This contrast provides an important key to the novel in terms of Tolstoy's distinction between head and heart. Whereas Kitty learns to live by her heart rather than by rational principles, Anna kills herself after hearing that reason can help us to escape, and Levin almost reasons his way to suicide. Though saved by the realization that true knowledge is beyond reason, he continues to search for a rational faith. As he puts it himself: "To me personally, to my heart, has been revealed a knowledge unattainable by reason, yet I stubbornly wish to express this knowledge by reason and in words" (9:415). Characteristically self-centered, he decides not to speak of this knowledge to Kitty because "it is a secret, necessary and important for me alone, and inexpressible in words." Whether this is true faith, he concludes, he does not know, but he will continue to pray even though reason cannot explain to him why he should.

Levin's inability to share his new insight with Kitty reflects an unresolved perspective on the question of how we should live at this point in Tolstoy's own life. The rather formulaic solution to marriage at the end of *War and Peace* gives way to questioning, even though we gain the impression that Kitty and Levin's marriage is a happy one.

The happiness that Kitty and Levin eventually find is anticipated in several ways. To begin with, each is remarkably sensitive to the other's feelings. Her desperate attempt to avoid hurting him when he proposes is soon followed by his instant recognition, from the involuntary brightening of her eyes when Vronsky appears, that she considers herself in love with this man.

Kitty and Levin are also revealingly vulnerable in their feelings about each other. When Levin arrives in Moscow to propose and Stiva suggests that he has entered an important new phase, "Levin suddenly blushed, not as grown-up people blush, faintly and hardly noticing it—but as boys blush, sensing that their shyness is amusing and therefore becoming ashamed and blushing still more, almost to tears" (8:27). Kitty blushes perhaps even more than Levin, and it is significant that she blushes "for Levin" early in the novel when he displays a lack of sophistication in conversation with Countess Nordston (8:63). This mutual vulnerability becomes more mirrorlike as the novel progresses. Levin later blushes "much more" than Kitty does when she tells him that she has encountered Vronsky. And as Kitty adds that she wishes he could have observed her conduct: "'I am now blushing much more—much, much more,' she said, blushing to tears" (9:261). Soon afterward, when it is Levin's turn to tell Kitty that he has met Anna, he blushes. Kitty is quick to wonder why, and as she questions him he blushes "still more" (9:292–93).

Kitty and Levin's ultimate happiness is also anticipated by the patterning of his perceptions of her at crucial moments in their lives. Early in the novel Tolstoy applies the word *mysterious* (*tainstvennyi*) continually to Levin's impressions of Kitty, her family, and love (9:29–31). Levin later attempts to plan his future life while gazing at the night sky. This night, he thinks, has decided his fate: his views of life have imperceptibly altered, like the cloud pattern in the sky. He terms this change "mysterious" concluding, of Kitty: "I love *her*" (8:305–6). Just before Levin makes his second proposal, he and Kitty "carried on a conservation, and it was not a conversation but some kind of mysterious communication" (8:428). Kitty and Levin are further united by his unique perceptions of her eyes, which he sees as "truthful" (*pravdivye*) in key scenes throughout the novel; for example, at the skating rink and during both marriage proposals. While Levin is observing the "mysterious" change in the night sky, a carriage passes by and two "truthful eyes" look out at him. We are told that this was Kitty only five lines later, but one could have guessed it by the adjective *pravdivye*.

"There were no other eyes like those in the world. There was only one being in the world capable of focusing for him the entire world and meaning of life" (8:305). Kitty's truthful eyes even have a mysteriously beneficial effect upon Levin, as when, late in the novel, he assures her that he has never felt their marriage could have been any better. He says this "not thinking" and just "to comfort her," but upon looking into Kitty's "truthful" eyes, he repeats it once more "from the bottom of his heart" (9:263).

Foreshadowings and Forces

Throughout *Anna Karenina* parallel incidents, recurrent images, and prophetic statements promote the impression that Fate plays a major role in the plot. This impression is reinforced by frequent suggestions that mysterious forces influence the attitudes and actions of the main characters.

Tolstoy associated the train with "unnatural" Western civilization. In 1857 he wrote in an unposted letter to Ivan Turgenev: "The railway is to travelling what the brothel is to love—just as convenient, but just as inhumanly mechanical and deadly monotonous."[20] Throughout *Anna Karenina,* trains are linked to disaster and death.[21] The death of a watchman, struck by a train at the time when Anna and Vronsky are first attracted to each other, combines with the strange dream that haunts both of them to foreshadow her suicide. (She herself terms the watchman's death a "bad omen.") Less obviously, the watchman's death in Part I and Anna's death in Part VII are both separately prefigured in miniature. In Part I, chapter 3, passengers fall from the roof of a "train," represented by a box in a game played by the Oblonsky children. In Part VII, chapter 19, Anna's son Seryozha describes to Stiva a train game in which the passengers may fall. As Seryozha says the word *fall,* Stiva notices that the boy's eyes resemble his mother's and asks if he remembers her. Deeply disturbed, Seryozha replies that he does not. In another subtle reinforcement of this foreshadowing, instead of the word *train* Seryozha uses the term *railroad* ("iron road" in Russian)—which (especially in view of the fact that the boy has already accurately predicted his mother's return) connects his prophetic game with the ominous iron image in the lovers' prophetic dream.

This dual dream is an essential component of the novel both artistically and psychologically.[22] It may be traced to the death of the peasant watchman, but in Vronsky's case it also reflects a recent experience during a bear-hunt. The man in his dream, evidently the beater at the hunt, is a small peasant with a tousled beard who is bending over doing something and mumbling in French. As Vronsky awakens, he feels an inexplicable horror (8:391). In Anna's dream, the same Russian words are used to describe the small, bent-over peasant with the tousled beard, and both she and Vronsky feel horror when she relates it to him. In her dream, however, the French words mumbled by the peasant are clear: *"Il faut le battre, le fer: le broyer, le pétrir . . ."* (8:397). This notion of striking iron becomes more clearly prophetic when Anna has the dream again prior to her suicide. In this version, a little old peasant man with a disheveled beard is bent over some iron, and she finally realizes the cause of her horror: "the peasant was paying no attention to her but was doing some terrible thing in the iron over her, was doing something terrible over her" (9:346–47). This final version most clearly anticipates Anna's death by the coldly impersonal train on the "iron road."

There are still other such foreshadowings in the novel. Early on, just before Anna meets Vronsky in the snowstorm, she sees "the bent-over shadow of a man" and hears "the knocking of a hammer on iron" (8:116). She then gets off the train and meets Vronsky, who declares his passion for her, whereupon the wind rattles a loose "sheet of iron." Before her suicide, Anna sees in her half-delirium a deformed peasant with mussed hair, bent over the wheels of the train. She finds "something familiar" about this peasant; then, recalling her dream, she trembles with fright (9:361). Finally, as she dies, we are told that "A little peasant man, repeating something, was working at the rails [literally, 'over the iron']" (9:364). The peasant figure working with iron stalks Anna in her adultery and appears like a sentinel of Fate at her death. In Gustave Flaubert's *Madame Bovary,* a blind man with a noisy stick performs a similar function.

Anna has two other prophetic dreams. Just before she gets off the train and meets Vronsky, she has a brief, half-delirious dream-vision. A peasant seems to be gnawing at something on the wall, an old woman grotesquely stretches her legs the entire length of the railroad car, and there is a terrible noise, as if someone were being torn apart. As we have seen, the peasant figure appears later, when Anna is in fact torn apart. The woman stretching her legs may be seen as a precognition of Anna's pain in childbirth, when she wants "only to stretch my legs a little."[23] Anna's dream that Karenin and Vronsky are simultaneously her husbands, as noted above, prefigures their actual appearance at her bedside, when she fears that she will die in childbirth.

Anna's death is foreshadowed in several ways by Tolstoy's treatment of Vronsky's horse, Frou-Frou. Dmitry Merezhkovsky has noted several elaborate parallels: Anna and the mare are similarly described in detail; Vronsky has a deep bond with both; he tragically contributes to each one's destruction. Perhaps Fate, Merezhkovsky concludes, sent Vronsky a warning in the death of Frou-Frou.[24] A parallel can also be drawn between Anna's pregnancy and Vronsky's kicking Frou-Frou in the belly after causing her fall. When his affair with Anna begins, we read that she would have fallen on the rug if he had not held her. It is then that he feels as a murderer must feel upon viewing the body of his victim. In a draft version of the novel, Anna bore the name "Tatyana" and the mare its diminutive, "Tanya." Tolstoy's choice of the name Frou-Frou was influenced by a popular French play in which the heroine, whose household name is Frou-Frou, deserts her husband and son to go off with her lover.[25]

In Part V, Anna's feelings toward Karenin are likened to those of a drowning person who survives by shaking off another drowning person. When Anna throws herself beneath the train, she is likened to a swimmer entering the water, and she throws down her red handbag. Not long before, Anna, frowning, had spoken of someone in a red bathing suit, then shaken her head as if driving away an unpleasant thought (9:336). In a draft version of the novel, Anna was to have drowned herself—an even clearer link with the fact that Frou-Frou falls at a water-jump, struggling like a fish.[26] Yet another connection between Anna and the mare is the fact that when Frou-Frou makes her fatal jump, she is likened to "a bird" and to a "wounded bird." In a later flashback, we learn that Anna "struggled like a captive bird" at that very moment.

Early in the novel Tolstoy has his characters unwittingly anticipate later events. When Anna arrives in Moscow, for example, Vronsky's mother tells her not to worry about Seryozha: "It's impossible never to be separated" (8:74). Immediately thereafter Stiva says of the watchman's fatal train accident: "Oh, what a horror! Oh, Anna, if you had seen it!" And when Karenin arrives at the steeplechase, Princess Betsy calls out to him: "I'm sure you don't see your wife. Here she is!" In *War and Peace,* Pierre receives an anonymous letter telling him he "sees poorly through his spectacles," for he alone does not know of his wife's affair with Dolokhov (5:25). Here, Karenin will see soon enough the alarm that Anna fails to conceal as Vronsky falls.

Still earlier, we learn that Vronsky has told Kitty that he never decides anything important without consulting his mother, and that he is awaiting her arrival as a "special happiness." Kitty attaches no particular significance to these words, but repeats them to her mother, who expects Vronsky to propose to Kitty and "knew that the old woman would be glad of her son's choice" (8:55). Since Vronsky then becomes passionately attracted to Anna at the station, his mother's arrival is indeed associated with a "special happiness" for him, and she is indeed "glad of her son's choice," at least for a while.

As we have seen, Dolly correctly predicts marriages, including Levin's to Kitty, and Seryozha predicts Anna's return. Other accurate prophecies turn on the use of the single Russian word *obrazuetsya* (something like "things will shape themselves" or "everything will turn out all right"). This word appears eleven times in the novel, in seven cases italicized; it is applied to four different troublesome situations and proves true in each one. First, the servant Matthew uses it in speaking of the bad situation between Stiva and Dolly. Stiva answers: "Do you think so? Who's there?" (8:12). It is Matryona, the children's nurse, come to urge Stiva to make peace with Dolly, and he agrees. A faintly eerie aspect of all this is that the expression *obrazuetsya* is really Matryona's own: we discover only much later, when she accurately applies it to Dolly's problems in the country, that "Matthew had taken it from her" (8:288). Stiva, who borrows it from Matthew ("A good little word . . . I'll have to use it"), applies it with remarkable success to an "unpleasant circumstance" connected with his new superior (8:411, 414) and to Levin's frantic problems with his clothing before his wedding (9:19, 20). The fact that Matryona had timed her beneficial appearance almost as if to promote the positive effect of her own expression adds a fateful tinge to its subsequent recurrence. In Anton Chekhov's novel *Three Years,* the hero Laptev borrows *obrazuetsya* from "Tolstoy's man-servant"[27] in speaking of his love for Yulia; like Levin, he then marries despite a refusal of his proposal, but his love for Yulia later diminishes.

Throughout *Anna Karenina,* characters seem mysteriously driven to act against their better judgment. When Dolly confronts Stiva concerning his affair with the French governess, he smiles stupidly and "entirely involuntarily," as we are told twice in one sentence. (The repetitions characteristic of Tolstoy's style are often eliminated in translation.)[28] At the station, Anna attempts to conceal her attraction to Vronsky, but it displays itself "irrespective of her will," even "against her will." At the ball, she smiles at Vronsky "involuntarily," attempting to hide the signs of joy that appear on her face "of their own accord."

Sometimes a single unnamed but apparently evil force influences Anna and others.[29] Anna first yields to it on the train from Moscow to St. Petersburg. After that, it aids her in deceiving Karenin, as when "she felt herself clothed in an impenetrable armour of falsehood. She felt that some kind of invisible force was helping and supporting her" (8:162). Shortly thereafter, Karenin himself is influenced by "the same spirit of evil and deception," and even Levin feels the mocking influence of "some kind of evil force" when he is close to suicide in Part VIII. The evil force that influences Anna is mentioned several times in the chapters leading up to her death; and just before killing herself, she apparently addresses this force, thinking: "No, I will not let you torture me" (9:363).

Connections

In a much-quoted letter of April 1876 to Nikolay Strakhov, Tolstoy declared, while discussing *Anna Karenina:*

In everything, or nearly everything I have written, I have been guided by the need to gather together ideas which for the purpose of self-expression were interconnected; but every idea expressed separately in words loses its meaning and is terribly impoverished when taken by itself out of the connection in which it occurs. The connection itself is made up, I think, not by the idea, but by something else, and it is impossible to express the basis of this connection directly in words. It can only be expressed indirectly—by words describing characters, actions and situations.[30]

One type of connection in the novel could be termed "transitional," for instance Anna's destroying her own marriage in the process of saving another one. When she returns home, Karenin wryly remarks: "Went with the mother, came back with the son." He then asks if many tears were shed at the parting, again unwittingly suggesting the developing alteration in her affections. Much later, Anna uses a photo of Vronsky to "push out" a photo of Seryozha from her album, symbolizing a shift of emphasis in her life.

Levin's brother Nicholas dies in Part V, chapter 20, which ends with the following statement about Kitty: "Her illness was pregnancy." Many have noted this terse juxtaposition of birth and death: there is a suggestion that one soul departs as the other arrives. Tolstoy reinforces this idea by likening Nicholas's agonies to birth pains ("His sufferings, regularly increasing, did their work of preparing him for death.") and by suggesting the departure of his soul from his body: Levin notices that "all day" the dying man "kept catching at himself as if he wanted to pull something off." In Part VII, when Kitty goes into labor, Levin notices that a candle is burning. Then, when Dmitry is born, his life is said to quiver like a little flame in a lamp. Anna later thinks "Death!" when a candle goes out in her bedroom; she then decides "to put out the candle" of her life, and as Part VII ends, her life is likened to a candle that flares up brighter and then goes out. Just as Kitty's pregnancy is linked to Nicholas's death, so Kitty's giving birth is linked to Anna's death.

Commentators have associated the "flame" of Anna's life with the "fire" of her passion for Vronsky. As we have already seen, she tries unsuccessfully at the train station "to extinguish" the gleam in her eyes, which "flared up" once again at the ball. In the sense that Anna's passion then becomes her life, it takes her life with it as it burns itself out. Images of heat, fire, and the color red recur at key points in Anna's life: the "red light" that "blinds" her just before she gets off the train and meets Vronsky in the snowstorm is actually a "red fire" in Russian. Sidney Schultze has determined that the following images recur in various clusters during key scenes in the novel: red, heat, light, train, French, peasant, falling, drowning, telegram, devil, and death.[31]

As in *War and Peace,* the French language often bears negative connotations. When Anna decides to commit suicide after hearing expressed in French the notion that reason is given us to escape our troubles, this can be seen as a fulfillment of the prophetic dream in which the peasant speaks French.[32] In *Anna Karenina,* the English language also frequently has ominous connotations. As Anna's ultimately fatal passion begins, for example, she admits to having "skeletons" in her closet; before her suicide, she thinks: "The zest is gone." Vronsky says "All right" just before the race in which he causes Frou-Frou's death, and Levin thinks of Kitty as "Tiny bear" before she refuses his marriage proposal. Inserted into the Russian text, such English words stand out slightly more than do French ones. However, it should be noted that certain other Russian words are merely said to be "in English" (for instance, Tanya's shouting that passengers have fallen from the toy train), just as the statement that reason is given us to escape our troubles is said to be "in French."

One connection throughout *Anna Karenina* forms a remarkable parallel between Levin and Pierre of *War and Peace:* these autobiographical figures are both repeatedly associated with bears. Prince Vasily refers to Pierre as "this bear" early in the novel (4:22). Shortly afterward Pierre, Anatole, and Dolokhov tie a bear and a policeman back to back. They put them into water, and the bear swims about with the policeman on his back (4:50). Pierre vividly recalls the incident prior to his duel with Dolokhov, who then suggests that Pierre himself is a "bear," fearsome, but to be hunted down in the duel (5:28). In *Anna Karenina,* Levin likes to hunt and kill bears; and the bear motif repeatedly links him with Kitty in rather unlikely ways. At the skating rink he recalls that he formerly called her "Tiny bear" and that she, with her two sisters, had been for him "the three bears" of the English fairy tale. (Since the words "Tiny bear" are given in English, it seems that Tolstoy was playfully referring to the three Behrs sisters, especially since Kitty is modeled after his own wife Sonya Behrs.) Later, during a hunt, Levin gazes at the stars of the Great Bear and then abruptly asks Stiva about Kitty (8:183). "Dim Arcturus" (the guardian of the Bear) is also mentioned, which suggests Levin and his interest in Kitty.[33] The Russian word *mrachnyi* ("dim"), which also commonly means "gloomy," aptly describes the mood of the "guardian" Levin: he is bracing himself for the news that Kitty has accepted Vronsky after refusing him. At the dinner just before Levin's successful proposal, Kitty mentions a bear he has killed and asks him if he has any bears on his lands. Tolstoy suggests that this had special meaning for Levin, even though there seemed to be nothing unusual in Kitty's words (8:422). In December of 1858, Tolstoy himself had killed a bear while bear-hunting; the next day another bear attacked him, biting him twice near one eye before he could escape.[34]

As various images recur throughout *Anna Karenina,* their interconnection becomes an essential component of its structure. In addition to trains (discussed above), a pervasive image is that of the sea. People are frequently described as sailors charting a course over the sea of life, sometimes seeking safe harbors or anchorage. They may also be fish: "Stiva, who gets along in society very well, is compared to a fish in water, while Levin, inept in high society, is a fish on land," one critic writes.[35] Of course the theme of drowning (also mentioned above) is related to the sea as well.

Anna's adultery is associated with two recurrent images: the removing of rings and the casting of stones. After her attraction to Vronsky has begun, she takes a ring from her finger and gives it to little Tanya Oblonskaya, who has been trying to pull it off. The notion of stoning an adultress comes from the Bible (John 8:7), and the image of casting stones recurs several times in connection with Anna.[36] Late in the novel Anna pulls her rings off and on as she imagines the effect of her death upon Vronsky, Seryozha, and Karenin. Vronsky then appears, and she tells him to "abandon" her (she uses the Russian word for "cast" [away]) because she herself has become a "stone" around his neck (9:339).

Episodes in *Anna Karenina* are also connected by what has been called "psychic linking."[37] Soon after Levin reads Tyndall's treatise on heat, for example, Anna feels very hot on the train. In two such cases, Levin himself makes the connection. As we have seen, he abruptly asks about Kitty after gazing at the stars in the constellation of the Great Bear. In the other instance, the mere mention of electricity (8:191) causes Levin to ask about Vronsky, who is repeatedly associated with electricity in the novel. When Levin and Vronsky first meet, the latter remarks that spiritualism may be a genuine but mysterious force like electricity (8:63). Humiliated before Karenin, Vronsky shudders as if hit by "a very strong charge of electricity" just before he attempts suicide.

Vronsky is also ominously associated with shadows. When Anna returns to St. Petersburg, Tolstoy writes that she has brought with her "the shadow of Alexey Vronsky" and that "a woman with a shadow usually ends badly." Before this Anna had recognized Vronsky in the snowstorm "despite the shadow in which he was standing." Other examples are the shadows that suddenly become animated as Anna imagines Vronsky's reaction to her death (9:346), and the shadow on the train platform in which he stands after her suicide (9:376).

The number seven is repeatedly connected with death in the novel, possibly because Anna Pirogova, the model for Anna Karenina, had arrived at the railroad station "at seven o'clock" and had thrown herself under "train number seven."[38] In the novel itself, Vronsky is given "number seven" for the race in which he causes Frou-Frou's death. This happens at apparently the seventh jump in the race (the jumps are not numbered), at approximately seven o'clock; Anna herself dies after seven in the evening, though no number is given for the train that kills her. When Stiva seeks out Levin at his hotel, he says: "Levin—number seven, eh?" Finding "number seven," he enters and exclaims: "Ah!

Killed it?," referring to a bear Levin has recently killed. They then discuss death at some length, as Levin declares that death haunts him (8:412–13).

In *Anna Karenina* more than any other work of his, Tolstoy established ominous conections between apparently insignificant details. An extreme example is the unlikely motif of hats. At the spa, Varenka is introduced as "the one in the hat like a mushroom" (8:241), and much later, her marriage hopes are shattered when she starts talking about mushrooms "against her will." This upsets Koznyshev, who is about to propose to her, and he too speaks of mushrooms "as if against his will." A few minutes later, he mentally reviews his planned proposal but then "unexpectedly" speaks to Varenka of mushrooms and never actually proposes (9:146).

Several other hat images contribute to the novel's general atmosphere of inevitable disappointment and, eventually, of doom. Before her suicide, Anna is jealous of Vronsky's attentions to a person twice described as "a young girl in a lilac hat" (9:347). As we have seen, Anna's incipient love for Vronsky is suggested by her revulsion at seeing her husband's gristly ears propping up the rim of his round hat. Before leaving for the steeplechase, she is disturbed to see "a black hat sticking out of a carriage and the all too familiar ears" of her husband, who, she resentfully fears, may "stay for the night" (8:227). Later in the novel, Vronsky twice removes his hat to wipe his head, and both times we are told of his increasing baldness (9:30–31, 211). Anna is later accosted by a man who raises "his shiny hat above his bald and shiny head" (9:355), whereupon she thinks to herself: "He thought he knew me. But he knows me as little as anyone else in the world." Anna then returns home, consumed with hatred for Vronsky: "Seeing his hat on the hook, she shuddered with revulsion" (9:356). Vronsky had left his hat behind once before—on the ground, when he realized he had caused Frou-Frou's death (8:222). Anna now goes off to her own death. Among other grotesque figures in the prelude to her suicide, she sees the attendant Peter, who "with an idiotic smile" raises his hat "as a sign of farewell" (9:360).

Chapter Six
Confession and Death

The treatment of death in Tolstoy's works can be viewed as a gradual clarification of some of his primary concerns. His two greatest novels are similarly Tolstoyan in many ways, but they are also revealingly different. Despite its emphasis upon death, *War and Peace* celebrates life; despite its moments of hope and joy, *Anna Karenina* darkly anticipates death. Prince Andrew's death, seen as a quite positive "awakening," contrasts sharply with Anna's ugly demise. Still more revealingly, only one of the five major characters in *War and Peace* (Natasha) attempts suicide, and she regrets the impulse in time to set her own recovery in motion. In addition to Anna Karenina's long-anticipated suicide, Vronsky tries to kill himself, and his going off to war at the end has been interpreted as a form of suicide; Levin is so close to suicide that he desperately avoids potential instruments of self-destruction; and both Kitty and Karenin experience despair little less intense than the sufferings of the other three. In short, the transition from *War and Peace* to *Anna Karenina* is a rather ominous one. The nature of the change can be suggested by asking whether the title *All's Well That Ends Well* could seriously have been considered for the latter novel, as it was for the former. Levin's agonized search for the meaning of life and his narrow escape from suicide lead directly to Tolstoy's *Confession*. Tolstoy had long focused upon the fear of death, especially upon the significance of how we face death and how this reflects back upon our lives, but now these concerns were to become a major moral theme of his literary work.

Confession

Though the censor banned Tolstoy's *Ispoved'* (*Confession*) in April of 1882, the work circulated in manuscript copies, one of which was read by Ivan Turgenev. In October of that year Turgenev wrote to author Dmitry Grigorovich that the *Confession* was "remarkable for its sincerity, truthfulness, and strength of conviction," but added that it "ultimately leads to the most sombre denials of all human life."[1]

Tolstoy added a two-page postscriptlike conclusion to his *Confession* in 1882, but the work was written essentially from his perspective of 1879. Having lived half a century, he divided his maturity into three segments: the years prior to his literary success, the period before marriage, and fifteen years of married life. His *Confession* opens with the frank admission that by the age of sixteen he had genuine faith only in self-perfection. He had ruefully noticed, moreover, that his attempts to achieve moral goodness were ridiculed. Perhaps still worse, his elders encouraged him to be ambitious, greedy, lascivious, and vengeful. Now at fifty, he recalled this early decade of his life with horror: "I killed people in war, challenged others to duels in order to kill them . . ." (16:110). Despite his "lying, robbery, lechery, drunkenness, violence, and murder," others praised him as a comparatively moral man.

Literary fame encouraged Tolstoy to adopt the values of his fellow authors, which, he eventually realized, were no better than his previous standards. He proudly assumed that he could promote "progress" by teaching men without knowing *what* to teach them. Six years passed in this way, save for two indelibly disturbing experiences: an execution he witnessed in Paris and the death of his brother Nicholas. "When I saw how the head parted from the body—both the one and the other thumping separately into the box—I understood, not with my mind but with my entire being, that no theories about the reasonableness of our existing progress could justify this deed" (16:113). His brother's death, Tolstoy adds, similarly exposed the inadequacy of a belief in progress as a guide to life. "A wise, good and serious person," Tolstoy wrote, "he fell ill while still young, suffered for more than a year, and died in agony, not understanding why he had lived and still less why he had to die."

After his marriage, Tolstoy declared, his efforts at self-improvement were focused upon securing the best possible life for himself and his family. However, he still did not know "how to live;" he was plagued by doubts about the meaning of life. His condition resembled that of a sick man who realizes that what he took for an indisposition is actually more important than anything else in the world—"death." His meaningless life had led him to an abyss of destruction: "All my strength drew me away from life. The thought of suicide came to me just as naturally as thoughts of how to improve my life had come before" (16:117). Tolstoy then recalled how he, like Levin in *Anna Karenina*, had avoided ropes and guns as seductive, almost irresistible temptations. Only the faint hope of finding some other answer, plus the fact that there would always be time for suicide, kept him alive. Yet he increasingly saw life as an evil and stupid joke, inevitably followed by stench, worms, and obscurity.

At this point, Tolstoy wrote, he resembled the traveler in an Eastern fable who was overtaken on a plain by an enraged beast. Climbing into a dry well, he clings to a branch growing from a crack on its side, while at the bottom a dragon waits to devour him. Two mice, one black and one white, gnaw at the branch, while the traveler licks a few drops of honey from its leaves. "So I too clung to the branch of life," Tolstoy explained, "knowing that the dragon of death was unavoidably awaiting me." The white and black mice of day and night kept gnawing at the branch, and the joys of life now failed to assuage his fear of the dragon: "Those two drops of honey which diverted my eyes from the cruel truth longer than the rest, my love of family and of writing— art as I called it—were no longer sweet to me." Both his family and his writing, Tolstoy sadly concluded, would necessarily end in death. He was then attracted even more strongly to suicide, because he could not answer the question, "Is there any meaning in my life that my inescapably imminent death would not destroy?" (16:122).

Tolstoy's desperate quest brought him to some discouraging insights. Socrates taught him that "the destruction of the life of the body is a blessing" (16:132). Schopenhauer contributed the notion that life is "that which should not be—an evil," and Solomon proclaimed that everything in the world is "vanity and triviality." Finally, Tolstoy formulated a view patterned on the words of Buddha: "one must free oneself from life."

The search for an answer among his peers also left Tolstoy bitterly frustrated. Though convinced that life is "an evil and an absurdity," he refused to seek escape in epicureanism. Yet he still declined to "end this stupid joke," hoping that his pessimism was somehow invalid. At last, again like Levin, he realized that a faith which "made it possible to live" was perhaps necessarily outside of reason. A turning to "unlettered folk" (pilgrims, monks, sectarians, peasants) seemed to confirm this. Finally, "a voice within" Tolstoy exclaimed that God is life: "Live seeking God, and then you will not have a life without God" (16:152). He was thus "saved from suicide," although he nevertheless concluded that the institution we call the Church has handed down to us both truth and falsehood.

Tolstoy completed his *Confession* in 1882 by describing a recent dream in which he seemed to find faith (16:163–65). The dream may be interpreted as a solution to the dilemma of the traveler hanging by a branch in the Eastern fable he had related three years earlier. Lying on his back in a bed suspended above a bottomless abyss, Tolstoy feared that he would tumble into the abyss. He then discovered that by "looking only upwards" (even though the space above was also "bottomless") he could overcome his fear: there was then "no question of falling." Even though it would make "no sense" if he were awake, he realized that at the head of his bed stood a slender pillar whose firmness "was undoubted despite the fact that there was nothing for that slender pillar to stand on." And just before Tolstoy awoke, a voice seemed to counsel him that if he continued to look up, his fear of death would not return.

Death as Intimidation

The perception of death as an inevitable, threatening presence goes back to young Nicholas Irtenyev's reaction to his grandmother's death in *Boyhood*. That reaction—"an oppressive fear of death"—is carefully distinguished from "grief" and seen as a vividly unpleasant reminder that "I too must die some day" (1:176). In *War and Peace*, this terrifying reminder evidently causes the coolly self-composed Prince Vasily Kuragin to break down and cry when old Count Bezukhov dies: "Everything will end in death, everything," he tells Pierre. "Death is terrible" (4:109). And in *Anna Karenina*, as Levin attends his brother, "death, the inescapable end of everything, confronted him for the first time with irresistible force" (8:383). "Levin now saw only death and the approach of death in everything," Tolstoy tells us. And later, when his brother does actually die, the Tolstoy-like Levin is haunted by a "still stronger" feeling of terror at the inexplicable inevitability of death (9:81).

This feeling of excruciating intimidation rose to a crescendo in the story "Zapiski sumasshedshego" ("Memoirs of a Madman"), written in 1884 and reworked several times during the next twenty years but published only in 1912. The tale reflects a nocturnal ordeal of Tolstoy's in the town of Arzamas, where, as he wrote to his wife in September of 1869, "suddenly I was overcome by despair, fear and terror, the like of which I have never experienced before. . . . May God preserve anyone else from experiencing it."[2]

As the story opens, the narrator tells us that he has been officially declared sane, although he has concealed his true feelings because an insane asylum would hamper his "mad work" (12:43). He is, however, convinced of his own insanity, whose roots he discovers in three child-hood experiences. First, when he was happily falling asleep at the age of five or six, confident of the harmony all around him, he had over-heard a domestic squabble that filled him with "cold terror." The child hid his head beneath his blanket, to no avail. Second, he recalls seeing a serf boy beaten by a man who kept strictly declaring "You won't." Though the boy said "I won't," the beating (and the refrain of "You won't") continued, causing the young spectator to undergo a second fit of near madness. Finally, the narrator's aunt told him about the per-secution of Christ. Unable to understand how His torturers could beat Him even as He forgave them, the lad sobbed and hit his head against the wall.

These three rather stylized episodes are linked by a common thread of anguish induced by man's inhumanity to man. Taken together, they suggest the beginning of a stark, moralistic parable. As John Bayley has observed of Tolstoy's fiction after his *Confession:* "His many meth-ods—his tentative plotting, his discursive variety—all give place to a single dedicated and selfconscious method."[3]

The narrator's symptoms of "madness" were temporarily suppressed, he suggests, by the sexual corruption of his youth. In his tenth year of married life, however, he experienced the first of three additional "at-tacks." On the way to purchase from a "fool" an estate "with large forests" he planned to sell enough wood from the rich forests on the estate to regain the purchase price—he stopped over at Arzamas. Dur-ing the night he was overcome with such uncanny horror that he des-perately wondered what its cause could possibly be.

"I am here," inaudibly answered the voice of death. A chill seized my flesh. Yes, death. It would come—here it was—but it ought not to be. . . . And this inner laceration was terrible. . . . In life there was nothing; there was only death, but it ought not to be. (12:47)

He began to pray, which helped only as a diversion, and then returned home without buying the estate.

The next attack of "Arzamas terror" occurred, appropriately enough, after he attended a performance of "Faust," when again he felt lacerated by the ominous presence of "death, the destroyer of everything." Again he vainly prayed for a solution to his agony, and his health deteriorated.

The final attack occurred while the narrator was out hunting in winter. "I had been a hunter all my life," he declares (12:51). The hunt is unsuccessful: the wolves break through the ring of beaters. On the trace of a hare, the narrator is again thwarted: "It jumped out so that I did not see." He turns back, but suddenly feels lost. Afraid of freezing, he turns back twice more, to be overcome by the same Arzamas terror, "but a hundred times worse." Shaking with fear, he wonders: "Is death here? I don't want it. Why death?" He prays again, though this time not to reproach God, but in the realization that he himself is guilty. He prays for God's forgiveness, and the terror soon subsides. At the same time he finds his way out of the forest: "I had not been far from the edge." Emerging, he returns home in a new "joyous" state and prays for forgiveness for his sins.

This third and last episode seems intended to be read metaphorically: the narrator, who has been "a hunter (or seeker) all his life," finally realizes (as he repents his sins) that he is close to the edge of the woods after all. Tolstoy's use of the forest to suggest that the narrator is (morally) lost is a nice touch, for it was by purchasing an estate "with large forests" from a "fool" that he had planned to take advantage of his fellow man. Moreover, the narrator's fear of freezing to death in the forest recalls the "chill" that had seized his flesh as he was on the way to buy the estate. It is even possible to interpret the uncontainable wolves as the narrator's former passions; the elusive hare that he "did not see" as the faith he had been vainly seeking; and the three times he "turns back" when lost in the forest as the three times he turns to God in prayer.

At the end of the story, the narrator refuses to buy another estate, "joyously" realizing that it is a sin to live on "the poverty and misery" of the peasants, "our brothers." This joyous feeling, we are told, marked the beginning of his true madness. Leaving church one day, he sees beggars at the exit:

And it suddenly became clear to me that all this ought not to be. Not only should it not have been, but it was not, nor was there death and fear, nor was my former laceration still within me, and I now feared nothing. Then the light fully illuminated me, and I became the way I now am. (12:53)

Giving away all the money he has with him, the narrator walks home on foot, talking with the people. Thus ends the parable: the narrator's "madness" is actually his enlightened understanding of the truth that we are all brothers, and the "mad work" to which he refers at the beginning consists of helping his fellow man. And as we also finally realize, the repeated phrase "ought not to be" precisely echoes the narrator's earlier reaction to the ominous presence of death, suggesting that just as he was lost when close to the edge of the forest, so was he also near to discovering the enlightened truth of brotherhood that destroys the fear of death and perhaps even death itself.

Death as Punishment

In Tolstoy's largely moralistic world, a life wrongly lived often ends in a tortured death. "I firmly believe that people are punished," Tolstoy wrote in 1907, *"not for their sins but by their sins."*[4] He wrote this to Mikhail Artsimovich, with whose wife his married son Andrey was having an affair. Tolstoy deplored his son's conduct, speaking of "its disastrous consequences whatever happens." A sinful course, he evidently believed, determines its own further path of suffering. Much of what befalls Anna Karenina illustrates this belief: her suicide can be viewed, quite simply, as the end of the inexorable earthly suffering that begins with her adultery. In his *Confession,* Tolstoy later declared that among the Russian upper classes, who spend their entire lives in idleness, amusement, and dissatisfaction, "a death without terror and despair is the rarest exception" (16:145–46).

In *Kreitserova sonata (The Kreutzer Sonata,* written 1887–89), Tolstoy presents contemporary upper-class attitudes towards sex and marriage as containing the seeds of death. Though somewhat deranged, the protagonist Pozdnyshev evidently expresses the author's own views, however extremely formulated. (In his afterword to the work, Tolstoy provided evidence that this was so.) After his wife courageously persuaded Alexander III to allow its publication in 1891, however, Tolstoy had strong misgivings about the story. There was "something nasty" in it, he wrote to Chertkov, "something bad about the motives which guided me in writing it, such bitterness has it caused."[5] Though *The Kreutzer Sonata* was justly criticized as one-sided and distorted, it has an infectious intensity (as Chekhov was quick to observe) that challenges the reader to deal with Pozdnyshev's arguments.

Essentially, the tale consists of Pozdnyshev's extensive, controversial explanation of why he killed his wife. He begins by declaring that what we call "love" is merely lust. "Spiritual affinity!" he scornfully exclaims. "In that case, why sleep together?" (12:130). Contemporary marriage, he contends, leads either to violence or deception; it often engenders "that terrible hell which causes people to become drunkards, shoot themselves, or kill and poison themselves and each other."

Pozdnyshev then relates the story of his life, portions of which resemble Tolstoy's other writings and reported descriptions of his own past. For example, Pozdnyshev's declaration that when taken to a brothel at age fifteen, he afterwards wanted to weep while still in the prostitute's room (12:135), parallels a similar one made by Tolstoy. And the insistence that the equation "beauty is goodness" is false (12:137) parallels a contention advanced early in *What Is Art?* When Pozdnyshev, just prior to marriage, shows his future wife the diary accounts of his former debauchery (12:138), one thinks of Levin in *Anna Karenina* and of the author himself as well.

Pozdnyshev likens the linkage between women and sex to that between the Jews and money: both have retaliated for their oppression by seeking sexual or financial control over others (12:144). He compares his own honeymoon, with its vulgar disenchantments, to the deceptions of a cheap side show. Sex, he concludes, is "not natural," and we should abstain from it, even though this would mean "the end of the human race." Can anyone, he asks, who looks upon the world doubt this? "It is just as doubtless as death" (12:147).

After the honeymoon, Pozdnyshev's marriage deteriorates still further, as increasingly frequent arguments lead to cold hostility. Their mutual hatred, he declares, was that of "accomplices in a crime:"

How is it not a crime that she, poor thing, got pregnant the very first month, and yet our swinish intercourse continued? Do you think I am digressing from my story? Not at all! I am only relating to you how I killed my wife. The fools! They think that I killed her then, with the knife, on the fifth of October. I killed her not then, but much earlier. The very same way that everyone now kills, everyone. . . . (12:151)

Pozdnyshev next deplores what he considers contemporary hypocrisy with regard to "women's rights." The failure of his marriage, he now admits, was not his wife's fault, for women's education will always depend on men's view of them. The only solution, he contends, is to alter the way men regard women and women regard themselves. Doctors also come in for harsh criticism, and Pozdynshev's attack on the "cynical undressing and feeling her everywhere" (of Pozdnyshev's wife by a doctor) recalls Kitty's plight as described early in Part II of *Anna Karenina*. Moreover, these "priests of science" show Pozdynshev's wife how to avoid having any more children. At this point she turns to music and becomes involved with Trukhachevsky, a violinist who accompanies her piano playing. Tolstoy himself had been stung, while courting Valerya Arseneva in 1856, by rumors that she had become amorously involved with her music teacher, and his wife Sonya in 1896–98 would develop a strange passion for the composer and pianist Sergey Tanaev. As Tolstoy did Tanaev, Pozdnyshev treated Trukhachevsky with exaggerated politeness; Pozdnyshev's wife may well have been as innocent of actual adultery as Sonya, though circumstances in *The Kreutzer Sonata* are suggestively compromising. The first epigraph to the story comes from Matt. 5:28, which says that any man who looks upon a woman with lust has already sinned with her in his own heart. The reader may be tempted to apply these words to Pozdnyshev's wife, though we see her suspicious responses to Trukhachevsky only through the eyes of her increasingly jealous husband. Pozdnyshev emphasizes that early in life he himself became depraved in his imagination, and that after sex with a prostitute he was "ruined forever." Edward Wasiolek even goes so far as to argue that "Pozdnyshev kills his wife not because she may have had an affair with Trukhachevski . . . but because he himself [Pozdnyshev] has slept with his wife."[6]

Pozdynshev tells us that the court eventually acquitted him as a deceived husband who had killed to defend his outraged honor. He insists, however, that "all husbands who live as I lived must either live dissolutely, separate, or kill themselves or their wives, as I did" (12:167). Both he and his wife, Pozdnyshev adds, had been on the verge of suicide. This may again remind us of *Anna Karenina* (even though Vronsky and Anna do not marry), especially since Pozdnyshev tells his story on the train and recalls that in his jealous despair he was strongly tempted to commit suicide by throwing himself under a moving railway car (12:185). One critic has called *The Kreutzer Sonata* "a gargoyle on the cathedral of *Anna Karenina*."[7]

Pozdnyshev's jealously reaches an extreme pitch as his wife and Trukhachevsky perform Beethoven's Kreutzer Sonata together, and his insistence that music mysteriously agitates the listener without any resolution (12:179) closely resembles a section of *What Is Art?* (15:181–82). The structure of Tolstoy's novel has been imaginatively related to Beethoven's sonata,[8] and readers of the story in English translation will probably not realize that just before Pozdnyshev kills his wife, the word "crescendo" is inserted in the Russian text to describe his feverish mood.

Pozdnyshev's murder of his wife, when he unexpectedly returns home late at night to find her at the piano with Trukhachevsky, is well prepared, and its description is vivified by Tolstoy's technique of "making strange." For example, Pozdnyshev recalls that as he wildly pursued his rival, "a weight" hung on his arm (12:191); the next sentence reveals that "the weight" was his wife. And though we have twice read of Pozdnyshev's intention to stab his wife in her side, the deed itself is graphically blurred: "I heard and remember the momentary resistance of her corset and of something else, followed by the sinking of the knife into something soft." As she dies, Pozdnyshev's wife tells him that she hates him, then cries out, "evidently frightened by something in her delirium." She tells someone or something to go ahead and "kill, kill" her, adding: "Only everyone, everyone, and him too" (12:196). These words echo Pozdnyshev's earlier assertion that he had killed her "the very same way that everyone now kills, everyone" and therefore reinforce his contention that contemporary upper-class attitudes toward sex and marriage contain the seeds of death.

In Tolstoy's story "Mnogo li cheloveku zemli nuzhno" ("How Much Land Does a Man Need?" 1886), the greed of a peasant is directly punished by death. The hero Pakhom purchases as much land as he can encompass on foot in a single day. His greed takes him too far, and though he races back to the starting point just before the sun has set, he drops dead from exhaustion. The answer to the title question thus becomes "enough to contain his body," enough for a grave.

The tale may be read as a Tolstoyan condemnation of land ownership, but it is also more carefully crafted than the critics have realized. After a public reading of the story at Moscow University, Tolstoy's wife wrote him: "the impression was that *the style* is remarkably austere, terse, not a single extra word; everything is true and precise, like a musical chord; there is much content, few words, and it is satisfying to the end."[9]

As the twelve-page story begins, Pakhom's wife is arguing with her sister, who is visiting from the city. Country life is difficult, she admits, "but we don't know anxiety." In the city, she claims, people either make too much or lose everything; moreover, city people are often tempted by the Evil One. Pakhom, who has been listening, emphatically agrees, adding that their only problem is a lack of land.

With enough land, he exclaims, he "wouldn't be afraid of the devil himself!" (10:358). The devil, who has been eavesdropping from "behind the stove," takes this boast as a challenge.

Already the main events of the story have been efficiently prefigured. Not only will Pakhom "know anxiety" as the Evil One tempts him, but the notion of making too much or losing everything accurately applies to his quest for land throughout the rest of the story.

As Pakhom obtains more and more land, it satisfies him less and less. Numerous references to his feeling "cramped" or "confined" (*tesno*) reinforce the irony (10:360–63) and perhaps also suggest the devil's influence: Pakhom's heart burns with desire as he feels cramped by lack of land. Tolstoy even puns upon the word when Pakhom quarrels with his neighbors: "Pakhom began to live on more spacious lands but in a more confined world." The ultimate irony of Pakhom's "confinement by land," however, is realized by his grave at the end, as he obtains "all the land he needs."

Learning that the Bashkirs will sell rich land for a low price, Pakhom visits them and strikes a deal with their Chief: "a thousand roubles for a day." As he encompasses the land, Pakhom will mark the corners by digging distinctive holes with a spade. However, if he fails to return to the starting point before sunset, he loses his money. That night in a dream Pakhom sees the Chief laughing loudly and holding his belly; thereafter he is transformed, in retrogressive succession, into two other men who figure in Pakhom's quest for more land and then finally into the devil, who laughs loudly over the prostrate body of a barefoot man wearing only trousers and a shirt. Looking more closely, Pakhom realizes that he is that man, and wakes up in terror (10:365).

The Bashkirs gather at daybreak on a small hill. Pakhom puts his money in the Chief's hat, set on the ground to mark the starting and finishing point. Armed with a spade, he sets off in the direction of the rising sun. After encompassing a great deal of fertile land and digging holes at the first two turns, Pakhom removes his boots to walk more easily. A second echo of his dream occurs after the next turn when he becomes fatigued and thinks: "If I lie down, I might fall asleep." As he walks on, it becomes "very hot"; "sleep" begins "to influence" him. The Russian word for "sleep" also means "dream," and it is used of the dream that Pakhom now seems to be reenacting. The extreme heat may further suggest the faint but increasing influence of the devil, who appropriately accepted Pakhom's "challenge" behind the stove and appeared in his dream.

Pakhom fights off the desire to sleep but walks on dangerously far to encircle some particularly rich-looking land before making the final turn. Seeing that the sun is now quite low, he digs a last hole and heads back towards the hill on which the Bashkirs await him. Realizing in horror that "the sun will not wait," Pakhom discards his extra clothes in further reenactment of his dream, keeping only the spade for support. As he dashes along, his "heart pounding like a hammer," he has an eerie feeling that death may be near. The setting sun now becomes "large, red, and bloody."

Pakhom rushes madly on, and the sun disappears. But he hears the Bashkirs shouting on the hill and realizes that there it is still light. With a last desperate effort he reaches the finish, where the Chief is laughing loudly and holding his belly. Recalling his dream, Pakhom collapses with blood flowing from his mouth. His grave is dug with the same spade he had used to make the holes marking the turns in his journey.

These holes, we see, were miniature suggestions that Pakhom in his feverish quest was digging his own grave, much as the "cramped" feeling that his increasingly spacious lands had ironically engendered in him is now realized in the confines of the grave itself. The image of the sun (which "will not wait") is particularly successful, as it races in its arching journey across the sky against the wide curve of Pakhom's greed upon the ground. He had decided, we recall, to set off in the direction of the rising sun. Later in the day, the sun's intense heat, recalling the devil's own element, appropriately "influences" Pakhom to lie down and sleep in a premature realization of his devil-induced dream. The fact that Pakhom's heart pounds like a hammer while the sun turns blood-red is a grimly apt anticipation of the blood that issues from his mouth as he dies. At the end, both Pakhom and the sun disappear beneath the ground after tracing their curving courses above the earth—a focus that appropriately reinforces the deadly playfulness of the story's title.

Death as Inspiration

Tolstoy's preference for the simple life of the peasants is reflected in his descriptions of their deaths. Thus in *Childhood,* the peasant woman Natalya Savishna "accomplished the best and greatest deed in this life: she died without regret or fear" (1:107). In his *Confession,* Tolstoy would write that unlike the nobility, the simple folk "approach death with tranquility, and most often with joy." This death, he concludes, is "the greatest happiness" (16:146). The Tolstoyan inference is that an unselfish, hard-working, natural life is rewarded by an inspiring, almost triumphant transition to the next world.

Even with this in mind, it is difficult to understand Tolstoy's story "Tri smerti" ("Three Deaths"), published in 1859. He worked especially hard on the story's ending (which features the death of a tree), but it puzzled many readers nonetheless. Ivan Turgenev wrote Tolstoy that "Three Deaths" was generally popular among St. Petersburg readers, "but they find the ending strange and don't even completely understand its connection with the two preceding deaths; those who do understand—are dissatisfied."[10] Some critics suspected that Tolstoy was losing his powers as an artist.[11] In a letter to Countess Alexandra, he attempted to explain the idea behind the story:

three creatures died—a lady, a peasant and a tree. The lady is pitiful and loathsome because she has lied all her life, and lies when on the point of death. Christianity, as she understands it, doesn't solve the problem of life and death for her. . . . The peasant dies peacefully just because he is not a Christian. His religion is different, even though by force of habit he has observed the Christian ritual: his religion is nature, which he has lived with. . . . The tree dies peacefully, honestly and beautifully. Beautifully—because it doesn't lie, doesn't put on airs, isn't afraid, and has no regrets.[12]

The three deaths seem valued in proportion to their closeness to nature. The "beautiful" death of the tree, as a part of nature itself, is better even than that of the "natural" peasant. Still, Tolstoy's explanation may not seem entirely satisfactory.

The story invites diverse interpretations. One of Tolstoy's best critics has observed: "The dying peasant who gives his new boots away, instinctively acts for the good of others."[13] But as another well-known critic has noted, this is "just not true," much as we would like it to be: the peasant grudgingly agrees only after he has been asked repeatedly, scolded for being wasteful, and promised a gravestone in return.[14] The second critic goes on to explain that the themes of class difference between peasant and noblewoman and of true and false Christianity are, like the excoriation of the hypocrisy attendant on the noblewoman's dying, invitations to misinterpret the story. This critic finds in it an "implication" (which he terms an outrageous violation of both Christian and humane feeling) "that compassion, grief, and pity are false." In support of this, however, he renders Tolstoy's opinion (in the above letter) that the dying tree "has no regrets" (*ne zhaleet*)[15] as "doesn't pity" (which the Russian could indeed mean, but which seems misleading in this context since it is the other trees which do not pity the dying one). He also appears to agree implicitly with Tolstoy that the death of the tree is beautiful because it "has no fear"—even though, as the first critic has noted, the author himself "appears to have forgotten" that in the story "he had described the tree as 'tottering on its roots in fear.'"

In view of such problems, "Three Deaths" should be interpreted cautiously, but it can also be seen, ultimately, as a suggestive exploration of the development of human life in its broadest natural context. The story is constructed upon contrasts within similarities. As it begins, we see the lady, who is pale, thin, and sickly, riding in a carriage with her maid, who is pink, plump, and healthy. The lady's hat, hanging inside the carriage, sways "before the nose" (3:59) of the maid. Yet when the edge of the maid's coat "barely touches" the lady's leg, she irritably pushes it away with the single word "Again," whereupon the maid moves further away, blushing furiously. They soon pass a church and the maid crosses herself. The lady is slow both to understand why and to follow her example.

These two initial themes—the clothing and the cross—recur in the story of the old peasant. As he nears death, a young peasant asks him for his new boots, which he will presumably no longer need. The old man agrees, provided that the young peasant buy him a gravestone. The young man later fails to do this, but does place a cross on the grave, for which purpose he cuts down the tree at the end.

The tree, then, is put to a useful purpose, like the new boots of the old peasant. Earlier, when the old man had been slow to part with them, the cook had reproached him by declaring that he had no "need" for them: he "will hardly be buried in new boots" (3:64). This point was important to Tolstoy. At the end of his story "Kholstomer" ("Strider"), a man is indeed buried in a new uniform and new boots (12:42). The man was "of no use to anyone," we learn, and yet his burial was "an extra difficulty for people." In sharp contrast, the body of the dead horse Strider is variously useful: people use his skin and his bones, and a wolf feeds his flesh to her cubs, who howl "joyously."

When the tree is cut down to make a cross at the end of "Three Deaths," the surrounding trees fill out the new space with their branches "still more joyously." And in the story's last sentence, these trees' branches and leaves rustle "joyously and peacefully" and "majestically." When the lady dies, her face is described as "stern, peaceful and majestic" (3:70). The carefully established contrast between "stern" and "joyous" reflects the contrast, as in "Strider," between a burdensome death and a useful one.

The tree's death, which Tolstoy called "peaceful, honest and beautiful," has a still greater, though also elusive, importance in the story. The cook, who had reproached the old peasant for being slow to give away his boots, has a dream which, she believes, foreshadows his death. In the dream he gets up from his sickbed and chops wood, saying that he wants to do something useful, whereupon the cook awakens to realize that he has just died. Though she does not know it then, her dream still more specifically predicts the death of the tree: the old man, she dreams, "seizes an axe" and "the chips fly all over." At the end of the story the young peasant "took his axe," and when he kills the tree "the chips were flying."

The peasant cook is thus attuned, through her dream, to the two deaths that Tolstoy viewed with approval. Another link is that the peasant's religion, in Tolstoy's words, is nature, and the tree, a part of nature, is carefully personified as it dies. First, we read that its leaves "whispered something," and a robin sitting on one of its branches moved to another tree. "The tree," we are told, "shuddered with its whole body . . . tottering on its roots in fear." Finally, "lowering its limbs," the tree falls to the earth, and "the robin whistled and fluttered higher." After this, the birds gather to "chirp something happy," while the other trees whisper joyously, peacefully, and majestically.

Whether or not one sees the hint of a departing soul in the robin that flies upward from the body of the dying tree, clearly nature itself is elaborately and even triumphantly personified by this "majestic" ending. Despite Tolstoy's apparent failure to remember the fear of the dying tree, the three deaths are admired to the extent they approach a harmony with the natural world around them. The death of the tree, as the surrounding trees "still more joyfully" fill out the new space with their branches, promotes this natural harmony. Attempting to answer the question "What is the aim of human life?" Tolstoy at nineteen had written in his diary: "If I begin with a view toward nature, I see that all within her is constantly developing and that each component part unconsciously facilitates the development of the other parts.

Man himself is such a part of nature, but endowed with consciousness; he ought then to strive, just as the other parts, consciously employing his spiritual faculties, for the development of everything in existence."[16] The fact that the tree in "Three Deaths" is used to make a cross, enabling one man to atone for his broken promise to another, makes the harmony of the tree's "beautiful" death particularly inspiring.

In "Alesha Gorshok" ("Alyosha The Pot," 1905), the death of a simple-minded, overworked peasant proves unexpectedly beautiful. The story's main theme is ironic offensiveness: Alyosha's nickname is a life-long reminder that as a child he had once broken a pot while running an errand. Continually mistreated, he worries most about offending others. The cook Ustinya is the only person who "pities" him, but their hopes of marriage are crushed as an offense to his employer and his father. When Alyosha injures himself fatally at work, he fears that "the master will take offense" (14:200). Before dying, he prays "only with his hands and his heart," feeling in his heart that just as this world is good if you obey and do not offend, so will all be good in the next one. As he dies, Alyosha is repeatedly "astonished at something." The subtle, touching implication is that his meek obedience and fear of offending others have finally been rewarded by an enlightened insight into the sacred value of his own goodness.

Death as Enlightenment

In Tolstoy's most famous short story "Smert' Ivana Il'icha" ("The Death of Ivan Ilych," 1886), the hero discovers a shattering truth just before he dies: his entire life has in a real sense been a protracted "death." Ivan Ilych is a sort of Russian Everyman whose disease is also deliberately generalized. As his surname Golovin suggests (*golova* means "head"), Ivan Ilych has functioned "from the head" rather than "from the heart." He has lived exclusively for his own pleasure, never questioning the value of such an existence. His striving toward the "pleasant" and the "proper" is relentlessly exposed as frivolous and false.

The repetitive pattern of Ivan Ilych's self-centered life is reflected in the circular nature of the story. For example, his daughter's fiancé is a court examiner, the same post Ivan Ilych himself held when he became engaged to his wife. Moreover, he "receives the same treatment from his doctor, when on trial for his life, as he himself had been accustomed to mete out to others in court."[17] In still another subtle circle, the odd taste produced by his medicine recalls one of the symptoms of the disease itself. Finally, after a painful, three-day struggle in a symbolic black sack (which has been likened to Jonah's three days of learning humility in the belly of the whale),[18] Ivan Ilych quite literally "sees the light." Comprehending the folly of his former existence, he thinks: "Death is over"—and dies.

The transformation of Ivan Ilych, who finally realizes that his life has been a sort of death, follows a simple formula: the concepts "pleasant" and "proper" are replaced by "pity" and "understanding." As his affliction worsens, he realizes that only his peasant servant Gerasim and his son Vasya "understand and pity" him (12:98). Just before his death it is revealed to him that his life was not what it should have been, but that this can still be remedied (12:106). He then begins to "pity" both his wife and son, as we learn from two short, separate sentences. Finally he attempts to express this "pity," but then breaks off, "knowing that the one to whom it mattered would understand." As Ralph Matlaw has put it: "The understanding Ivan Ilych reaches and the pity that he feels are contrasted with his inability to communicate and his indifference whether he does, and the discovery that his salvation no longer depends on external expression but on inner conviction."[19]

Deciding, in his new compassion for his wife and son, to relieve both them and himself of suffering, Ivan Ilych abruptly discovers that pain, and even death itself, seem to be vanishing.

There was no fear whatsoever because death, too, was no longer.
In place of death there was light.
"So that's what it is!" he announced aloud. "What joy!" (12:107)

All of this strongly recalls the narrator's "joyous" experience at the end of "Memoirs of a Madman," when his fear of death disappears as he sees the "light" of the brotherhood of man. Ivan Ilych's enlightenment, however, is merely a hopeful component of his inexorable death.

In "Khoziain i rabotnik" ("Master and Man," 1895), Tolstoy's tale of two men lost in a snowstorm, the hero who "sees the light" acts nobly before he dies. Having tried to abandon his servant Nikita in an attempt to save himself, the merchant Brekhunov then dies while us-

ing his own body warmth to save Nikita's life. The story has been
demonstrated to contain symbolic echoes of Christ's passion, including
the crowing of a cock, a Peter who turns away, and even Brekhunov's
crucifixlike posture during his self-sacrificing death.[20] Most contemporary readers were deeply moved by the hero's change of heart, though
one critic complained that if Brekhunov indeed forgot about himself
and thought only of Nikita (as Tolstoy tells us), the exploit was too
unexpected and unmotivated.[21]

On the other hand, John Bayley argues that Tolstoy renders the merchant Brekhunov's noble impulse "both moving and convincing" by
using business-related images to describe his thoughts and actions.[22]
For example, Brekhunov warms Nikita in order to save his own life as
well: he acts "with the same decisiveness with which he used to clinch
a good business deal" (12:337). Nevertheless, one could disagree with
Bayley's opinion that the merchant remains true to his "nature and
personality" throughout the story. After Brekhunov has sheltered Nikita's body with his own, he is "amazed" by "a joy he had never before
experienced." Tears fill his eyes, and he soon thinks "neither about his
own legs nor about his own arms, but only about how to warm the
peasant lying beneath him." The goodness of Brekhunov's deed thus
seems to acquire an unexpected momentum capable of transcending
selfish calculation. Though he now thinks "boastfully," as in concluding a business deal, that he is saving Nikita, Brekhunov soon has a
dream in which his new feeling of joy is said to be "completed"
(12:339): he is summoned by the one who bade him lie down upon
Nikita. "I'm coming!" he cries "joyously"—and "awakens, but awakens not at all as the same person he was when he fell asleep." Indeed,
Brekhunov now exhibits an attitude toward his servant that he could
presumably never have felt before: "and it seemed to him that he was
Nikita, and Nikita was he, and that his life was not in his own self,
but in Nikita." Tolstoy obviously intended to demonstrate that Brekhunov dies a transformed person, fully aware of a sacred bond with his
fellow man.

Brekhunov's dream, in which his new joy is "completed" by the
realization that he has been motivated to save Nikita by the one who
is now summoning him, exemplifies Prince Andrew's idea (in *War and
Peace*) that "God is love" and that, as a particle of love, man returns to
the eternal source at death. As he dies, Prince Andrew realizes that
"death is an awakening." In a letter of 1892, Tolstoy expressed his own

belief that "death is an awakening." Our life, he explained, is like a dream compared to "the more real, actual, true life from which we come when we enter this life, and to which we return when we die. . . . But even that truer life is only one of the dreams of another, still truer life and so on to infinity, to the one last true life, the life of God." Tolstoy knew this "for certain," he declared: "when I die I shall rejoice that I am waking up to that more real world of love."[23]

Chapter Seven
Resurrection

Tolstoy wrote his third and last major novel during the years from 1889 to 1899. The basic plot line had been suggested to him by the eminent jurist A. F. Koni during a visit to Yasnaya Polyana. A young orphan girl was brought up by a rich lady who gave her some education but kept her as a servant. Seduced at sixteen by one of the lady's relatives, the girl was driven from the house; she placed her newborn child in an asylum and became a prostitute. Later she was accused of stealing money from a drunken man in a brothel. On the jury that heard the case was the young man who had originally seduced her. Overcome by remorse, he married her, but she died of typhus soon after her four-month prison sentence expired.[1]

The story moved Tolstoy deeply, especially since as a young man he himself had seduced a servant girl named Gasha, though with far less tragic consequences. While working on the novel, he accepted an advance of twelve thousand roubles from the publisher in order to provide aid for the Dukhobors, a persecuted religious sect. Tolstoy's wife, who counted upon such money for much of the family income, was particularly offended that her husband, as she saw it, was describing his own unsavory past with undue relish. She had seen "this very Gasha," she wrote in her diary, and her husband, in portraying the hero Nekhlyudov "as progressing from his downfall to his moral resurrection, . . . thinks this very thing about himself."[2]

A moralistic and didactic novel, *Resurrection* condemns virtually all the established institutions of church and state. In the powerful Toporov—whose name suggests an "axe" and who is described as "devoid of moral feeling" (13:305)—one detects a portrayal of the Church's high official Konstantin Pobedonostsev.[3] The censor required numerous alterations in the text, yet it is surprising that publication was permitted at all. In R. F. Christian's words:

The belief that all judgment is not only useless but immoral . . . that men in authority . . . are inevitably corrupted by the power they exercise . . . that the organized church has made a mockery of Christ's teaching and lent its authority to everything from the incantation over the bread and wine to the practice of war, capital punishment and all forms of legal constraint and violence . . . that taxation is robbery . . . that educated society is for the most part selfish, venal and hypocritical; that sexual relations are frequently degrading and offensive to human dignity; and that only when . . . all acknowledge their guilt before God, . . . learning to respect and love as Christ (not the church) enjoined them will there be any prospect of founding the kingdom of heaven on earth—all these beliefs are gathered together in one place, and expressed in *Resurrection* with an uncompromising and dogmatic vehemence.[4]

Though by no means as great a work as *War and Peace* and *Anna Karenina*, *Resurrection* was received enthusiastically. Some readers viewed the novel as an ominous portent, appearing as it did at the transition point between two centuries. Soviet critics have predictably interpreted it as a wholesale indictment of Russia before 1917. *Resurrection* also returns to many of Tolstoy's early themes and concerns, carrying them to, and perhaps even beyond, their logical extremes. The hero is the same Dmitry Nekhlyudov who was a close friend of Nicholas Irtenyev in *Childhood, Boyhood, and Youth,* where, as John Bayley has noted, Dmitry's sister had called him "an egoist . . . [who] in spite of all his cleverness [was] very fond of admiration."[5] Now, in *Resurrection,* Prince Nekhlyudov struggles to eliminate the element of self-satisfaction from his own process of moral regeneration.

The Meaning of Resurrection

Tolstoy's title *Voskresenie* means both "Resurrection" and "Sunday" in Russian: Nekhlyudov seduces Katyusha on Easter Sunday night. Earlier that evening she had greeted him with the traditional *"Khristos voskrese"* (Christ is risen), and he had made the accepted reply *"Voistinu voskrese"* (Truly, He is risen). In view of this association, the title refers primarily to Nekhlyudov's decision to atone for his sins and to begin a new, truly moral life, as well as to the initially painful but ultimately beautiful change he then helps promote in Katyusha. However, the theme of resurrection, both actual and potential, runs throughout the entire novel, which begins with four epigraphs from the New Testament.

From the very beginning *Resurrection* reminds us of Tolstoy's earlier works. A passage explaining the way Nekhlyudov's attempts at self-improvement were thwarted by the people around him recalls Tolstoy's

Confession. His efforts to be good, Tolstoy tells us, were ridiculed, while his lapses into vice were encouraged. In a particularly ironic touch, he tells us that when he wished "to remain a virgin until marriage, his family feared for his health" (13:53). When he first meets Katyusha, Nekhlyudov's perceptions of her are described in terms recalling those used of Levin's impressions of Kitty early in *Anna Karenina:* "As soon as Katyusha would enter the room or even when Nekhlyudov saw her white apron from afar, everything would become illuminated for him as if by the sun" (13:50). And when he returns, three years later, the mere sound of her voice causes a sun to seem to appear as if from behind clouds (13:56).

Early in the novel Tolstoy repeatedly emphasizes the duality of his hero. In Nekhlyudov, he declares, there were two beings: the spiritual and the animal. When he first met Katyusha, his spiritual self had defined the nature of their relationship, but three years later, his animal self was in control, and he reminds us of the hero of *The Kreutzer Sonata:* Nekhlyudov is "a depraved and accomplished egoist who loved only his own pleasure" (13:52). But when he sees Katyusha again his spiritual self revives, and during the two days before Easter he experiences a continuous inner struggle (13:58). Yet Nekhlyudov's animal being seems destined to win, for we are repeatedly told that he has ceased "to believe himself." The clear inference is that Nekhlyudov has become so "depraved" that his animal self cannot help but betray his true, or spiritual, self. This betrayal is accompanied by a repeated crowing of cocks as he goes to Katyusha at night (13:67): the crowing of a cock is associated with Peter's betrayal of Christ.

Nekhlyudov recalls this betrayal of his spiritual self seven years later at Katyusha's trial, when he "felt fear, as if he had not come to judge but to be judged" (13:71). Moreover, the image of illumination by the sun associated with his perception of Katyusha is replaced, after the seduction, by his awareness of "something dark and menacing" in the distance (13:68). He recalls this "something" in the courtroom, when he fears that Katyusha has recognized him (13:73).

After Katyusha is unjustly sentenced to penal servitude in Siberia, we are told that "the spiritual self, which alone is true, powerful and eternal, had awakened in Nekhlyudov" (13:108). He resolves to change his way of life, beg Katyusha's forgiveness, and help her in any way possible, including marriage. Tears appear in his eyes—tears, Tolstoy tells us, "of tender emotion over his own self, over his own virtue." This intrusive feeling of self-satisfaction, which suggests that his resurrection is by no means complete, recurs several times before Nekhlyudov succeeds in visiting Katyusha in prison. As he begins speaking to her, the thought of his own righteous remorse once again causes tears to appear in his eyes (13:152). But when he begs Katyusha's forgiveness and offers help, Nekhlyudov is shocked by her reaction: she is apparently so depraved that her only desire is to use him in any way she can, as her provocative smiles now suggest. Moreover, his appearance has revived memories that she had wished to forget. When he later proposes to Katyusha, her reaction is still more disappointing: "You enjoyed me in this life," she angrily exclaims, "and now you want to use me for salvation after death!" (13:173) Tolstoy then explains the painful impact this has upon both of them: "Had he not tried to expiate, to atone for, his deed, he would never have realized the extent of his transgression, just as she would not have become aware of all the evil done to her."

Katyusha spends the money Nekhlyudov gives her on vodka and keeps refusing his offers of marriage, but a glimmer of hope suddenly appears. When Nekhlyudov reaffirms his intention to follow her to Siberia, she shyly offers to stop drinking in order to please him. Still later, as she comes to believe in his resolve, Katyusha continues to try dissuading him, but her eyes say "something entirely different," and her entire face shines with joy (13:251). He now senses that her resurrection has at last begun:

He knew only one thing—that she had altered and that an important change was taking place in her soul, and this change united him not only with her but with Him in Whose name that change was being made. And this very union brought him to a state of joyous agitation and tenderness. (13:252)

Tolstoy then artfully prepares the reader for what is perhaps the novel's most touching scene. Having obtained a transfer to the hospital for Katyusha, Nekhlyudov gives her a photograph from their past, which makes her see the terrible contrast with her present position and to focus upon its cause. The vivid recollection of past happiness gives rise to a new surge of bitterness: "She would have broken her word and started drinking again if she had been in prison," Tolstoy tells us. "Here, however, liquor could only be obtained from the medical assistant, and she was afraid of him because he had been pestering her."

Returning from St. Petersburg, where he has failed to obtain a modification of Katyusha's sentence, Nekhlyudov is deeply hurt to learn that she has been sent back to prison for lewd behavior with the medical assistant. Upon visiting her he "coldly" remarks that the affair was "her business" (13:316), but pity soon overcomes his wounded pride and he once again declares his resolve to stand by her. "It's useless," she answers, but her face is radiant. Nekhlyudov then leaves, feeling a quiet joy, peace, and love for everyone that he has never before experienced. "Let her carry on with the medical assistant—that's her business: he loved her not for himself, but for her and for God."

Only at this point do we learn that Katyusha has been unjustly accused of carrying on with the medical assistant: in actual fact, his forceful advances had caused a commotion which had led to her return to prison. She had wished to tell Nekhlyudov the truth, but when she tried "she had felt that he did not believe her, and that her excuses would only strengthen his suspicions: tears choked her, and she was silent." Katyusha's inability to defend her innocence is thus delicately balanced by Nekhlyudov's valiant attempt to forgive her uncommited crime. She is now in love with Nekhlyudov again, Tolstoy adds, and makes every effort to improve because she knows he wishes it. Katyusha persistently refuses his offers of marriage, however, because she does not want to cause him unhappiness. Yet the possibility that he could think she had behaved badly in the hospital is said to torture her more than does her sentence of penal servitude.

Soon afterwards an entry in Nekhlyudov's diary reads: "Katyusha does not want my sacrifice. She wants her own" (13:335). He is overjoyed, he adds, at the "inner change" taking place in her: she seems to be "coming back to life." Her resurrection thus merges with his own. As Nekhlyudov follows her to Siberia, he repeatedly notices that "inner change," which results in "a feeling he had never experienced before." He no longer experiences self-satisfaction, but simply "pity and tenderness, not only towards her, but towards all people" (13:383). By this time, Katyusha's resurrection is also virtually complete, although some details—the sudden austerity of her face, or her apparent aversion to all possible signs of coquetry, which recalls a similar didactic emphasis in *Family Happiness*—may strike us as moralistic. Katyusha's final decision to remain with the prisoner Simonson instead of marrying Nekhlyudov is rather patly interpreted by the latter as proof of her sacrificial love for him.

The theme of resurrection is variously suggested and sustained throughout the novel. The first sentence describes shoots of green grass which appear in spring despite the efforts of people to block their path with stones. This image of grass shoots rising despite stones is echoed as Nekhlyudov leaves to visit Katyusha in prison (13:146), where he sees a large picture of the Crucifixion (13:148); the reader may thus be intended to recall that Christ arose despite a large stone blocking His tomb. Later, as Nekhlyudov follows Katyusha to Siberia, he regrets that stones prevent the ground from giving birth to grass and other growing things (13:361). People ignore what "God has written" in their hearts—they are hardened against compassion as these stones are against vegetation, he thinks.

The idea of people ignoring what God has written in their hearts is further reflected in Tolstoy's bitterly ironic references to Christ and His resurrection. An Englishman who inspects a squalid prison but still believes in its value asks Nekhlyudov to tell the prisoners (in Russian) "that Christ pitied them, loved them, and died for them. If they believe this, they will be saved"(13:447). When Nekhlyudov sees the picture of the Crucifixion in Katyusha's prison, he reflects that it should be associated with liberation rather than imprisonment. In another prison he finds a large image of Christ, "the inevitable accessory of all places of torture, as if in mockery of His teachings" (13:188).

Still another reflection of the theme of resurrection occurs in the story of Theodosia, which Nekhlyudov hears on his way to Siberia. This young woman is jailed for attempting to poison her husband, Taras, but then released on bail at harvest time. As they reach the house, Theodosia begs Taras to forgive her. "I myself didn't know what I was doing," she says. "I forgave you long ago," he answers simply. (Here we may note that the novel's first epigraph strongly urges forgiveness.) Theodosia works so hard at harvesting that everyone is astonished: she seems a totally transformed person, and very close to Taras, as if they were both "one soul." Formerly, she admits, she had not wanted to live with Taras, "but now," she tells him, "you're in my heart!" (13:368). Though they had both soon forgotten her crime, she was sentenced to servitude in Siberia, and Taras is now following her there, as Nekhlyudov is accompanying Katyusha. Theodosia's resurrection can thus be seen to parallel and to reinforce Katyusha's, with the difference that Katyusha quite literally "did not know what she was doing" when she administered the poison, since she apparently believed it to be a sedative.

The Evils and the Remedy

Resurrection is a book-length indictment of man's inhumanity to man. Virtually all social conventions and institutions are methodically, viciously exposed as evil. The hero's diverse experiences afford Tolstoy ample opportunity for this, particularly as Nekhlyudov struggles to work within the system, as one of its privileged members, to right its injustices. The extreme position at which he arrives at the end has, in his view, been fully justified by his experience.

The novel's opening paragraph suggests that people are blind to beauty and goodness, preferring instead to cheat and enslave one another. Katyusha, after her seduction and pregnancy, is obliged to become a prostitute, to take up "that life of chronic crime against human and divine law" which "the government not only permits but sanctions" and which "ends for nine out of ten women in painful disease, premature decrepitude, and death" (13:15). As Katyusha's trial begins, the prosecutor turns out to be poorly prepared because he has spent the night at the very house of prostitution where she had formerly worked. The judge, moreover, is impatient to get the trial over with, since his mistress can meet him at a hotel only until six o'clock. When this same man slightly bunches up the embroidered sleeves of his official uniform, "exposing heavily hairy arms" (13:32), we are provided a vivid metaphor for much of the novel.

The priest then swears in the jury, as he has done countless times without realizing that he is "leading people in taking oaths over the Gospels in which oaths are forbidden." Tolstoy now employs his technique of "making strange" to vivid, didactic effect. In demonstrating how to raise the right hand, the priest positions his fat fingers as if taking "a pinch" of something. The members of the jury repeat the oath in an awkwardly unsynchronized chorus, holding their "pinches" aloft in solemn awe "as if fearing that they might drop something" (13:34). Here the pious empty pinch is to religious dogma what the exposed hairy arms are to hypocritical legal oppression. The prison church service (described in Part I, chapters 39–40) carries Tolstoy's indictment to an almost self-defeating extreme. He repeatedly suggests, for example, that to consume bread and wine made God's flesh and blood is a form of cannibalism and a blasphemous mockery of Christ. The gilt cross that the priest holds out for the people to kiss "was nothing but a representation of the gallows on which Christ had been executed precisely for forbidding what was now being done in His name" (13:144).

Like the clergy, the medical profession indulges in routine charades. Early in the novel Tolstoy describes the government officials—male doctors—who examine prostitutes once a week and clear them "to continue their crimes" (13:15). These men, "sometimes stern and serious, sometimes playfully merry, destroy all barriers of shame given by nature not only to people but to animals." Later on, a Siberian officer, laughing unpleasantly, assures Nekhlyudov that female prisoners are thoroughly searched.

Throughout the book Tolstoy stresses the fact that Nekhlyudov had been brought up to be a hypocritical seeker of pleasure. Even his own mother was rather pleased when he became "a real man" by stealing a French woman from one of his friends. It is thus a nice touch when he recognizes Katyusha in the courtroom through his "pince-nez" (the word is in French in the Russian text), which he then puts on to conceal his tears of remorse.

When Nekhlyudov seduced Katyusha, he was a young officer proud of his depraved existence. The fact that an officer must be prepared to sacrifice his life, Tolstoy declares, convinces him that a dissolute life is "not only excusable but even essential" (13:55). And what lies ahead for some of these young officers? While seeking aid for Katyusha's fellow prisoners, Nekhlyudov visits an influential general who had received a coveted decoration in the Caucasus "because under his leadership, close-cropped Russian peasants dressed in uniforms and armed with rifles with bayonets had killed more than a thousand people who were defending their freedom, homes and families" (13:274). Later, Tolstoy adds, this man had forced Russian peasants to commit many different crimes, and now he was highly respected. When an orderly brings him Nekhlyudov's visiting card, the general is absorbed in spiritual communication with the soul of Joan of Arc. Needless to say, he is more interested in his spiritualism than in the prisoners, and so responds to Nekhlyudov's requests with indifferent references to rules and regulations. "There are no innocent prisoners," he tells Nekhlyudov. "We know them well."

A major target of Tolstoy's in *Resurrection* is the legal system itself, which Nekhlyudov at one point describes as "an administrative weapon" to benefit the upper class (13:332). Tolstoy reinforces this indictment with several ironies. Katyusha's sentence results from a miswording of the jury's verdict, and Nekhlyudov fails to notice the error because he is so upset by the injustice of her entire situation. His attempt to have the sentence appealed fails because the man who casts the deciding vote considers Nekhlyudov's "determination to marry this girl in the name of moral imperatives to be repulsive in the highest degree" (13:286). Still another remarkable consequence of the legal system is that a man who should have been sentenced to penal servitude has been appointed governor of a town in Siberia. As we learn much later, he is the only one there who refuses to accept bribes.

Throughout the novel Tolstoy directs his scathing satire at such diverse subjects as duels and fashionable social chatter. Hearing two people discuss a new play, Nekhlyudov realizes that they are interested neither in it nor in each other, "and if they were talking it was only to gratify the physical need after eating to move the muscles of the tongue and throat" (13:101). He also hears of an officer killed in a duel after another officer had said "something uncomplimentary" about his regiment while they were both drinking and eating oysters. Tolstoy later stresses the fact that had "the murderer" acted otherwise than he did, his fellow officers would have expelled him from their regiment. This leads Nekhlyudov to compare "the murderer's" fate with that of a peasant who had also killed a man after heavy drinking: the peasant was in chains, separated from his wife, and condemned to hard labor, while the officer would be confined to a comfortable room for a few days, to drink wine, eat good food, and read books, and then be set free to live as before, having become "especially interesting" as a result of his duel (13:269).

Tolstoy devotes a considerable portion of the novel to condemning the private ownership of property. As George Steiner has suggested, Nekhlyudov's "return to the land" is the physical correlative to the rebirth of his soul.[6] His frustrated efforts to improve the lot of his peasants recall those of Prince Dmitry Nekhlyudov[7] in *A Landowner's Morning*. Influenced by the writings of Herbert Spencer and Henry George, Nekhlyudov visits his estates and attempts to draw up legal agreements to benefit the peasants. Despite his careful explanations, the peasants are suspicious in direct proportion to his generosity: they view Nekhlyudov as "the master" who can do whatever he pleases in any case, and so they interpret his mysterious offer as a clever swindle. Even his steward misunderstands Nekhlyudov's intentions, because the idea that "every man is concerned only about his own profit at the expense of other people" is "so deeply rooted in the steward's consciousness" (13:228). Failing to discern any such profit, the steward is relieved to "understand" that Nekhlyudov is not in his right mind. Tolstoy soon amplifies this notion by having Nekhlyudov hear about a rich landowner with softening of the brain who gave his lands to his peasants with disastrous consequences (13:244).

As Nekhlyudov follows the prisoners to Siberia, Tolstoy variously "makes strange" the cruelty of their treatment. Unaccustomed to physical exercise, several of them collapse from standing and marching in the blazing sun: their deaths are considered "annoyances" in contrast with the "tragic" injury of a horse. To Nekhlyudov, the prisoners seem "not people, but some sort of peculiar, frightening beings" (13:340). Two children in a "fine carriage" also watch the procession: one fearfully concludes that the prisoners are bad people who must be dealt with in this way, but the other realizes "directly from God" that they are being deeply wronged.

There is little need to dwell upon the prisoners' sordid living conditions: the common expression "feeding lice" signifies "being in jail." Disease often goes untreated, food and clothing are inadequate, the air is putrid, and toilet facilities are not picturesque. There are "noseless" people among the prisoners, and Tolstoy explains that their nostrils have been torn off as a form of punishment. Nekhlyudov's agonized observation that these people are being murdered without anyone's knowing who is doing it (13:359) recalls the questions that plague Pierre in *War and Peace* as the French mechanically execute Russian prisoners.

Nekhlyudov's conclusion that "mutual love between people is the fundamental law of human life" (13:362) is the first major step toward answering the question that has haunted him for some time: "By what right do some people punish others?" (13:323).

Nekhlyudov obtains partial answers and insights from three people he meets on his journey to Siberia. The first is Simonson, the man with whom Katyusha remains in the end. While still a schoolboy, Simonson had decided that the income of his father, a quartermaster, was dishonestly earned and should be given away to the people. He was later arrested for expressing unorthodox views. Though he declared that the judges had no right to condemn him, Simonson was exiled to Archangel province, where he formulated the doctrine "that everything in the world is alive, that nothing is dead, that all the objects we consider dead or inorganic are in reality parts of an enormous organic body which we cannot comprehend, and that man's task, since he is a particle of this organism, consists of supporting the life of this organism and all its living parts" (13:381). Tolstoy had expressed strikingly similar ideas in his diary at the age of nineteen.[8] In accordance with this doctrine, Simonson opposes "war, capital punishment, and every kind of killing, not only of people but of animals." As for sexual relations, Simonson believes that "procreation is only a lower function of man; a higher one is to serve those who are already alive." This idea, so point-edly relevant to both Nekhlyudov's past and present, also recalls the views of Pozdnyshev in *The Kreutzer Sonata*.

The peasant Nabatov, another intelligent prisoner, constantly mulls over the question of how best to live in this world. He carries "in the depths of his soul the firm, peaceful conviction common to all laborers on the land" that "nothing ceases to exist, but constantly changes form—manure into grain, grain into a hen, the tadpole into a frog, a caterpillar into a butterfly, an acorn into an oak—and so man is not destroyed, but only undergoes a change" (13:405). Nabatov loves work, bears hardships easily, and does not fear death. The fact that his "firm, peaceful" outlook is related to his working on the land may recall Nekhlyudov's own "return to the land" during the early stages of his resurrection.

The views of a "shaggy old man" termed "good-for-nothing" and "crazy" are clearly applicable to Nekhlyudov's own life. As John Bayley has observed, it is difficult not to see "in this apparition the aged Tolstoy."[9] The old man declares that he has "no faith at all," and so believes "no one except myself" (13:431). This interests Nekhlyudov, who suggests that the self could be mistaken. The old man disagrees. People adopt different faiths, he explains, because they believe others, and not themselves: "If everyone believes his own spirit, all will be as one." These words echo Tolstoy's narrational observation that Nekhlyudov seduced Katyusha because he failed "to believe himself," be-traying, instead, his "spiritual self" by heeding only his "animal" one. The old man claims that he is "persecuted like Christ," and later tells Nekhlyudov that in the prisons "the servants of the Antichrist are feed-ing lice with people" (13:451).

In Siberia Nekhlyudov concludes that all the evils and crimes he has witnessed are not caused by "degeneration" or "chance" or some "crim-inal type" (as "dull-witted scholars" claim in support of the govern-ment), but rather that they are "the inevitable consequence of the incomprehensible delusion that some people may punish others" (13:426). This conclusion is based upon five rather cynical observa-tions. From among free people, he decides, the courts and the admin-istration select for incarceration "the strongest and most gifted," for they are also more "hot-tempered" and less "crafty" than others. These people are then subjected to such "unnecessary indignities" that they retain almost no motivation for goodness. In addition, they face such dangers that even the kindest among them resort to cruelty for the sake of self-preservation. Moreover, they are corrupted by being compelled to live with others who have themselves been corrupted by life. Finally, they become indelibly convinced that the extreme cruelty of their treatment is officially condoned whenever it benefits the government. "It is just as if a project had been assigned to find the best and surest method of depraving as many people as possible," he concludes in horror.

The remedy that Tolstoy's Nekhlyudov discovers at the end of the novel also comes in five parts, and it is related to the answer that Christ gave to Peter: "we should always forgive everyone even an infinite number of times because there are no people who are not themselves guilty, and therefore none can punish or correct others" (13:455). We thus revert to the novel's first epigraph, which emphasizes forgiveness, the main theme of the five "commandments" of Tolstoy's hero. First, we should not only not kill, but not even be angry at our fellow man. We should refrain from adultery, and also from binding ourselves by oaths. Fourth, we should "turn the other cheek," humbly forgiving all offenses against us. Finally, we should love, help, and serve our enemies. Only if these commandments are followed, Nekhlyudov concludes, "will the greatest blessing for man be attained—the Kingdom of Heaven on earth."

Suggestive Images and Backgrounds

As we have seen, Tolstoy uses three details during Katyusha's trial (Nekhlyudov's pince-nez, the priest's "pinch" of something, and the judge's exposed hairy arms) to evaluate various aspects of the proceedings. *Resurrection* contains a variety of such images, some of which recur to form vividly suggestive backgrounds.

The second and third epigraphs to the novel condemn hypocritical behavior, something the hero is trapped in when we first meet him. Nekhlyudov rejects the idea of private property but needs the income from some recently inherited estates for his routine extravagances. He hopes to end an affair with a married woman, but she wishes to continue it. He wants to avoid marrying Missy Korchagin, a possessive girl he has been weakly courting. He had wished to become an artist, but discovered he lacked talent. On his easel stands an unfinished painting—literally "a turned-over begun picture" (13:21)—which appropriately suggests his desire to rid himself of these two women. However, it still more aptly symbolizes his shameful seduction of Katyusha, which, as we soon learn, has been such a "turned-over begun picture" for seven years.

When Nekhlyudov arrives at his aunts' estate prior to his seduction of Katyusha, she brings him "a piece of scented soap, just removed from its wrapper" and two towels: "Both the untouched soap with its imprinted letters, and the towels, and she herself—all this was equally clean, fresh, untouched, pleasant" (13:57). Much of this description quite pointedly anticipates the seduction, especially as she herself is likened to the untouched, uncovered, pleasant soap she brings to him in his bedroom.

In the flashback describing the summer when Nekhlyudov first met Katyusha, they play *gorelki*—something like "catch" or "tag." After several rounds, they become partners and run together. "Well, there's no way to catch those two now," says the young artist who pursues them, "unless they stumble" (13:49). After this, they come to

a flowerbed with lilac bushes behind which no one ran, but Katyusha, glanc-ing back at Nekhlyudov, gave him a sign with her head to join her behind the flowerbed. He understood her and ran behind the bushes. But here, be-hind the bushes, there was a small ditch, unfamiliar to him and overgrown with nettles; he stumbled into it and, stinging his hands on the nettles and getting them wet with the fresh evening dew, fell, but instantly, laughing at himself, he righted himself and ran out onto a clear place. (13:49–50)

The notion that no one will "catch" Nekhlyudov and Katyusha in the game unless they "stumble" anticipates the loss of innocence in their relationship and its consequences. The "sign" that she gives him "with her head to join her" suggests that she will attract him physically to seduce her. The "unfamiliar" ditch is quite literally an unanticipated "pitfall," after which Nekhlyudov's conscience will prick him like the nettles. His "fall" further suggests his "sin." His righting himself and running out onto a "clear place" anticipates his self-justification after the seduction ("everyone does it") as well as his quick disentanglement; the word "clear" (*chistoe*) also means "clean" and is later used to describe Katyusha and the soap and towels.

In the game, we are told, Katyusha soon "moved up close to" Nekh-lyudov, who, "not knowing himself how it happened," kissed her "on the lips." This innocent encounter anticipates the dangerous events of three years later: her coming to his room; the kiss he gives her there, contrasted with "the unconscious one behind the lilac bush" (13:64);

and finally, his strange state prior to the seduction, when he comprehends very little of what is happening.

After Katyusha's trial, Nekhlyudov goes to the Korchagins' for dinner, where Missy presses him to agree that "nothing reveals a person's character as much as a game" (13:98). They converse with her mother, who remarks to Nekhlyudov that a trial must be very depressing for anyone "with a heart." She makes another unwitting indirect reference to Nekhlyudov's personal life by asking about the picture he is painting, which he says he has "completely abandoned." In the Russian, his answer is, literally, "abandoned her" (the word for "picture" is feminine), which further links the "turned-over begun picture" to his seducing, and then abandoning, Katyusha. "You shouldn't have!" Missy's mother tells him, and then reproaches Nekhlyudov for not revealing his true feelings in their conversation. He suggests that this is possible only "in a game" (13:103). Later on, Nekhlyudov guiltily thinks that Katyusha will soon be going away to penal servitude and decides that he cannot continue his empty way of life, for then he "would be continuing his picture, which, clearly, would never be finished" (13:125).

Tolstoy makes one more explicit reference to the game of *gorelki,* and in so doing appropriately introduces another suggestive image. Before leaving for Siberia, Nekhlyudov returns to the estate he has inherited from his aunts, where he sees lilac in bloom "just as it was fourteen years ago when he played *gorelki* behind that lilac with eighteen-year-old Katyusha and, having fallen, got stung by nettles" (13:215). Nekhlyudov's steward then invites him into his office but disappears after "smiling as if promising something special with that smile." There is whispering behind a partition, followed by silence. Soon a barefoot peasant girl in an embroidered blouse and wearing earrings passes by the window.

As he leaves for the village after talking with his steward, Nekhlyudov meets the girl with the earrings. When he returns in the evening, the steward proposes dinner "with a particularly joyful smile," mentioning that the girl with the earrings had helped his wife prepare it. The dishes are served by "the frightened girl with the earrings," while the steward smiles "even more joyfully," ostensibly proud of his wife's cooking skill. That is all. Nekhlyudov does not respond to this frightened, dressed-up girl, but it seems clear that she has been readied for "the master's" enjoyment, particularly since his past involvement with Katyusha was undoubtedly common knowledge among the peasants.

In *Resurrection* Tolstoy uses a favorite thematic detail—the window—
in a new way: to focus the intense emotions of Nekhlyudov and Katyusha when they are separated from—and look in or out upon—each
other. The first time it underlines his lust for her and her fear of him.
Before the Easter night seduction, Nekhlyudov leaves the house and
walks to the window of the maids' room with pounding heart. A small
lamp is burning inside, and Katyusha sits pensively at a table. Her
face betrays an intense inner struggle; his pity for her only intensifies
his desire. When he knocks at the window she starts, as if from an
electric shock, then comes to the window and recognizes him. Katyusha seems to foresee what will happen, and her expression is "unusually
serious." Even her smile is a reproach: "in her soul there was no smile—
only fear" (13.67). Nekhlyudov motions to her to come out, but she
shakes her head and remains by the window. He presses his face to the
pane and starts to call to her, but someone distracts her from inside,
and he walks away. After stepping in several puddles, he returns to
knock on the window again. This time she opens the door, and they
kiss passionately.

Several months after the seduction, Katyusha learns that he is passing through on the train. It is a rainy night, but she walks to the
station and looks through the window of his first-class carriage
(13:136). Two candles are burning near the window. Nekhlyudov sits
there laughing, and she knocks on the window with a hand numb from
cold. Someone else rises and looks out. She knocks again and presses
her face to the window, but the train begins to move. Nekhlyudov
tries to lower the window as she runs along desperately beside the
departing train. In despair, she thinks of him drinking and laughing
in his velvet armchair while she remains, soaked and muddy, in the
cold night. Her idea of throwing herself under the next train vanishes,
however, when her baby suddenly moves within her.

The two nocturnal scenes are strangely symmetrical. In the first, he
presses his face against the window as she sits beside a lamp; in the
second, she presses her face against the window to see him sitting near
two candles. He steps in puddles, she is soaked with rain, and each
knocks two different times to attract the other's attention. Also in both
cases, feelings of love outside the window are brutally overpowered: he
is seized by intense lust, she by jealousy, even hatred.

In the third episode, Katyusha is leaving for Siberia while Nekhlyudov looks into a train window at her. Locating the cars for women
convicts, he puts his face to a barred window (13:352) and attracts

attention. Katyusha comes to the window and takes hold of the bars: "Sure is hot," she says, smiling joyfully. He says he will try to have water brought for her, and adds that they will not see each other until the next station. "Are you really going?" she asks, "as if she did not know this," joyously looking at Nekhlyudov. He assures her that he is, and she requests that a woman who is in labor and groaning with pain be left behind. He tries to arrange this, but the convoy officer declares: "Well, let her be in labor. We'll see later on." Then Nekhlyudov watches the train leave: the men's cars roll past, he hears the groans of the woman in labor, and finally he sees Katyusha standing at the window "smiling pathetically at him." In this third window episode, the tortured, rough emotions of the two earlier ones yield to tortured but tender mutual affection. Both are experiencing their own resurrections, and they feel a new closeness to each other even as they become temporarily separated. All this is the more touching as the groans of the woman in labor in this railroad scene recall the inner stirring of Katyusha's baby that once kept her from throwing herself under the next train.

Tolstoy also made use in *Resurrection* of what might be termed interspersed suggestive background details. In *Childhood*, as Boris Eikhenbaum has observed, "gestures and movements are broken up into separate moments, run parallel to the conversation and form an entire system."[10] In the example he gives, a conversation between Nicholas Irtenyev's parents is interspersed with remarks and gestures involving the passing of a pie at dinner. In *Anna Karenina* Tolstoy developed this technique further by making the interspersed background details evocatively pertinent to a given situation. When Karenin confers with a lawyer about a divorce, their conversation is interrupted by moths that keep appearing, some of which the lawyer catches. The moths are appropriate because the conversation is a stuffy one and because Karenin is himself helplessly caught in a delicate situation. Later, when Levin, feverishly jealous, asks Vasenka Veslovsky to leave his home, his angry remarks are interspersed with descriptions of his breaking a stick into splinters with his bare hands. In *Resurrection* Tolstoy utilizes this characteristic technique to intensify the scene preceding the Easter seduction. As Nekhlyudov leaves the house at night, we are told that "strange sounds" were being made by the breaking up of ice on the river (13:66). Watching Katyusha through the window of the maids' room, Nekhlyudov hears the pounding of his own heart "together with" these strange sounds: "There, on the river, in the mist, some kind of slow, ceaseless work was going on; something would wheeze, then it would crack, then it would shatter, and thin fragments of ice would ring like glass." The near personification ("wheeze") of the breaking ice is particularly effective because the inner barriers between Nekhlyudov's spiritual self and his animal one are completely breaking down. As Katyusha recognizes him at the window, "on the river was occurring the very same strange wheezing, rustling, cracking and ringing of the ice." Finally, after he has possessed her, "below, on the river, the cracking, ringing and wheezing of the ice became still more intense, and to these previous sounds a murmuring was added." Just at this moment the "something dark and menacing" appears.

At another point, when attempting to help Katyusha, Nekhlyudov visits a senator named Volf, who agrees to recommend a review of her sentence. He stresses, however, that the senate cannot be swayed by the particular nature of the case, and looks gravely at the ash of his cigar (13:267). When Nekhlyudov suggests that this case is exceptional, he responds:

> "I know, I know. All cases are exceptional. We shall do our duty, and that is that." The ash was still holding on, but had begun to crack and was in danger. "Are you seldom in Petersburg, then?" said Volf, holding his cigar to keep the ash from falling. But the ash started to shake, and Volf carefully carried it to an ashtray, into which it finally fell.

As this background vividly suggests, the possibility of a pardon for Katyusha is quite precarious. In fact the senate is indeed unswayed by the nature of the case, and hope, like the delicate ash, crumbles and falls.

Not all of the suggestive images Tolstoy uses in *Resurrection* are so artistically satisfying. Deep in the novel, when Nekhlyudov joyfully decides to keep on helping Katyusha, something flashes in the sky "above his very head," followed by a roar of thunder (13:234). And just after he arrives at the conclusion that any crime can be callously committed if one fails to love one's fellow man, a rainbow appears on the horizon (13:361). At such moments, as George Steiner phrases it, "the tract invades the poem." And yet, despite the "puritanical conception of art" embodied in *Resurrection,* he adds, it contains "wondrous pages" and "moments in which Tolstoy gave rein to his unchanging powers."[11]

Chapter Eight
Tolstoy's Vision, Values, and Art

Had Tolstoy been resurrected fifty, sixty or seventy years after his death, he would probably have been both horrified and grimly gratified. He would have noted that he had correctly foreseen the violence and bloodshed of the Bolshevik revolution, as well as the triumph of commercial vulgarity throughout the West. Like Solzhenitsyn, he would have had little sympathy for either of the two superpowers and the condition of their peoples, the one (as he would most likely have seen it) choking inexorably in its own freedom, the other "correctively" threatened by hard labor, torture, and drugs. In Tolstoy's play *I svet vo t'me svetit* (*The Light Shineth in Darkness*), a believer in nonviolence who refuses to serve in the military is incarcerated as a lunatic; in *Resurrection,* the hero's efforts to give up his ownership of private property are considered insane.

Tolstoy would very likely have sympathized with the rebellions of the 1960s and 1970s, from the antiwar movement to peaceful back-to-the-earth campaigns. He vehemently opposed capital punishment, and warned against the potential dangers of scientific and technological progress. He also anticipated the modern emphasis on physical fitness, vegetarianism, concern with the damage done by smoking and drinking, the demystification of church ritual, and the supposedly newly discovered science of "body language." Some of his descriptions of moribund states are strikingly similar to what have later been investigated and termed NDEs, or near-death experiences. It has even been convincingly argued that Tolstoy's case in favor of a radical change in men's outlook on women and women's way of regarding themselves is remarkably similar to the feminist arguments of the late 1970s.[1]

Tolstoy would also have felt at home with the modern interest in Eastern philosophy, including the concept of karma. As we have already noted, there are similarities between Tolstoy's theory of historical causation as set forth in *War and Peace* and Taoist teachings; and Pierre's dream of the globe of drops may be likened to the Taoist doctrine that

123

at death one is reabsorbed into the total flow. In a letter of 1892 elucidating "the Buddhist concept 'karma,'" Tolstoy affirmed his personal belief in Prince Andrew's revelation that "death is awakening" and that as a particle of love, we return, at death, to God, the original source of love. And in Tolstoy's story "Karma" (1894), we read: "To consider oneself a separate being is an illusion. . . . 'He who harms others, does evil to himself. He who helps others, does good to himself'" (12:272).[2]

By the age of nineteen, Tolstoy had carefully formulated his conviction that the aim of human life is the comprehensive development of mankind as an integral, perfectible component of the entire universe, a belief that may yet prove the most remarkable testimony to his awesome vision. Theoretical physicists and cosmologists such as Freeman Dyson, Alan Guth, Marc Davis are only now discovering more and more instructive connections between the largest bodies and smallest particles in the universe, connections suggesting that the universe may well resemble a giant brain pervading the cosmos, observing itself, and deliberately ordering the works of nature. Tolstoy's descriptions of fateful moments in which people think of themselves as insects, specks, or atoms and yet see their destiny in the vault of a lofty sky reflects an intuitive understanding of the purposeful development of the cosmos. And the fact that in experiments of quantum mechanics, electrons may be viewed as having the "free will" to choose direction (even though the choice seems to us determined only by probability) may yet throw some analogously corroborative light on Tolstoy's discussion of human free will in the second epilogue to *War and Peace.* Less speculatively, the beliefs of Simonson, Nabatov and "the shaggy man" in *Resurrection* may be combined to suggest that all existing things are part of a (literally) universal evolution. In Simonson's view, man is merely a particle in an enormous organism, parts of which, like the earth's crust, we erroneously consider to be inorganic. Nabatov is persuaded that nothing ever ceases to exist but only changes form, and he has no fear of death. The shaggy man insists that if everyone acts in accordance with his true inner self, "all will be as one."

Tolstoy's prodigiously energetic development is often seen as the result of a ceaseless struggle between two inner titans: the creator of immortal prose, who triumphed before the *Confession* (1879); and the fiercely moralistic prophet who generally won out therafter. Yet his life was also purposely unified. Both in life and in art, he never ceased to search for an answer to the question of how we should live. But that is precisely where the conflict began. Not only were some of Tolstoy's powerful instincts continually at war with his ideals; his attempts at self-perfection led to insights—for example, "happiness consists of living for others"—which caused difficulties and disillusionments reflected throughout his quite autobiographical fiction.

When he was twenty-six, Tolstoy recorded in his diary his hope of founding a practical Christian religion, one "not promising future bliss, but realizing bliss on earth."[3] In his fiction, this ambition was ultimately reflected in the five "commandments" proposed at the end of *Resurrection* as essential for creating a Kingdom of Heaven on earth: he thought he needed a set of rules, a code to live by. However, Tolstoy did depict in his art a single supreme human virtue, which we have termed spontaneous altruism in this study.

The ability to provide immediate, selfless aid to those in need is perhaps best exemplified by Natasha and Pierre in *War and Peace* and by Kitty in *Anna Karenina*. The main stumbling blocks are calculation, which thwarts spontaneity, and self-involvement, which vitiates altruism. As Tolstoy's autobiographical heroes reason their way toward virtuous behavior, they frequently fall prey to self-satisfaction.

Spontaneous altruism is depicted in Tolstoy's works as a primarily female virtue. Natasha and Kitty possess an instinctive ability to comfort and help others, acting more "from the heart" than "from the head." In a critique written in 1906 of Chekhov's story "Dushechka" ("The Darling") Tolstoy went so far as to extol Chekhov's rather empty-headed heroine who selflessly lives for others. "The author obviously intended to ridicule this rationally (but not emotionally) pitiful creature," he wrote. However, she is "not ridiculous but holy." Women, he concluded, are superior to men not only in their motherly abilities, but in their capacity for "doing that which is highest, best, and brings a person closest to God—loving and devoting yourself completely to the one you love" (15:316–7).

Pierre is thus a truly exceptional Tolstoyan figure: a male hero who instinctively comes to the aid of others. However, in his natural humility, he must outgrow the conviction that one can attain happiness through a plan of living for others. Like Natasha and especially like Kitty, Pierre exhibits most of his spontaneous altruism after passing through intense personal suffering. In the story "Chem liudi zhivy" ("What People Live By"), three people with their own troubles nevertheless give aid to others, and the reader is urged to conclude that we live by allowing the love that is God to function through us in this way.

After great personal suffering, Pierre spontaneously offers to Natasha (following her attempted suicide) a love that almost literally brings her back to life. She later does much the same for her mother after Petya's death. It is of course a Tolstoyan irony (like Anna Karenina's destroying her own marriage while trying to save another's) that Pierre, while trying to assassinate Napoleon, saves both the Armenian girl and the child in the Moscow fire. However, these spontaneous acts of heroism also set Pierre apart as a truly exceptional hero. Levin (in *Anna Karenina*) and, for that matter, Dostoevsky's famous "positively good man" Prince Myshkin (*The Idiot*) do not act in this way. Indeed, not only do Prince Myshkin and Dostoevsky's other "positively good" hero, Alyosha Karamazov, perform remarkably little active good; both may even be accused of failing to prevent a murder.

Isaiah Berlin introduces his perceptive argument that "Tolstoy was by nature a fox, but believed in being a hedgehog" with a quotation from the Greek poet Archilochus: "The fox knows many things, but the hedgehog knows one big thing."[4] These two distinctive traits are surely of crucial importance in any attempt to understand Tolstoy. In his almost obsessive, lifelong search for the One Truth, his natural inclinations frequently seem to be those of a hedgehog. One thinks, for example, of Tolstoy's claim that after more than sixty-five years he still believed in the existence of a single secret that would enable people to live in perfect health and harmony (the secret, he had been told as a child, was inscribed upon a green stick and buried in the Zakaz forest); or of Ivan Turgenev's condescending accusation made early in 1857: "God grant that your mental horizon may grow wider with each day! Systems are valued only by those who fail to lay their hands upon the whole truth, who wish to catch it by the tail; a system is indeed the tail of truth—but truth is like a lizard: it will leave its tail in your hand and run away, knowing it will soon grow another."[5] Isaiah Berlin goes on to contend that Dostoevsky's distorted interpretation of Pushkin as the bearer of a single Dostoevskian message neglects the protean genius of that arch-fox Pushkin, while demonstrating that Dostoevsky was himself "nothing if not a hedgehog." Tolstoy's transformation of that other arch-fox Chekhov into a Tolstoyan moralistic message-bearer is quite similar.

To be sure, Berlin focuses primarily upon Tolstoy's art. Just as Tolstoy was a fox attempting to be a hedgehog, he contends, so "his gifts and achievement are one thing and his beliefs, and consequently his interpretation of his own achievement, another."[6] But Tolstoy the artist—especially in his depiction of reasoning to extremes—also seems strikingly like a hedgehog. In *Childhood,* young Nicholas decides that the phrase "like our own dear mother" (in his poem for his grandmother) "clearly proves" that he has never loved his own mother and has even forgotten her. In *Youth,* he maintains that "the very fact of declaring a good intention makes it difficult—and even for the most part impossible—to carry out that good intention." In *War and Peace,* Pierre decides that when he said *"Je vous aime"* to Hélène, it was "a lie, and still worse than a lie" (5:34). And in *The Kreutzer Sonata,* Pozdnyshev advances the notion that we should abstain from sexual relations even in marriage, and even if that would mean the end of the human race.

It can be argued that such statements, made by generally autobiographical figures, are more representative of Tolstoy himself than of his art as such. The fact is that such extreme viewpoints emerge in the author's narration as well. In *War and Peace,* for example, he constantly repeats the notion that so-called great people actually have the very least influence on historical events. And in *Anna Karenina,* which convincingly depicts the perceptiveness of children, the author declares that dissembling may deceive the most intelligent person but not "the most limited child." As George Steiner has observed of Tolstoy's art: "Whatever he wrote seems to have, in Keats's phrase, a 'palpable design' upon us. The act of invention and the impulse towards instruction were inseparable."[7] If this is so, Tolstoy's hedgehog tendencies were more basic than were his foxlike ones. We should shift the emphasis of Berlin's valuable interpretation slightly to see Tolstoy as a natural hedgehog with foxlike tendencies: having methodically developed an idea to its extreme, he would then discover a new truth, also soon to be reasoned, relentlessly, to its own extreme.

The controversial essay *What Is Art?* reveals both the power and the limitations of Tolstoy the hedgehog. Indeed, this work treats established art in much the same way that *Resurrection* does the establishments of church and state. Condemning all established art as elitist and corrupting, Tolstoy proposes four criteria as the measure of true art: it should be sincerely felt, convincingly presented, widely accessible, and promote goodness. Ideally, the most limited peasant would appreciate such art fully, and be a better person for having done so. Thus, a theatrical performance by a primitive tribe that evokes compassion in the audience for a young deer, wounded by a hunter, is emphatically better than Shakespeare's *Hamlet,* which Tolstoy dismisses

as a "false imitation" of genuine art (15:163). Also dangerously false
are voluptuous or esoteric paintings, as well as classical music, which
combines these two aspects of bad art by arousing nervous agitation in
unhealthily educated listeners without satisfying it (15:181). In *The
Kreutzer Sonata,* classical music is presented as an evil, hypnotic force.
How can the presto of Beethoven's work "be played in a drawing-room
among ladies in low-necked dresses?" asks the ultimate Tolstoyan
hedgehog Pozdnyshev (12:180).

What of Tolstoy's own art? Does it satisfy the exacting demands of
his iconoclastic essay? His works written before the *Confession,* as Tolstoy himself sadly insisted, most assuredly do not. Yet his masterpieces
mostly belong to that period. Tolstoy's art after the *Confession* does tend
to conform more to his eventual theoretical requirements, but even
then not entirely. John Bayley has cautiously suggested that in terms
of Tolstoy's own theory of art, "Master and Man" may be "the most
impressive story" he ever wrote.[8] A good case can also be made for
"What People Live By," even though it was not an original story.[9]

What, then, are the essential elements of Tolstoy's greatness as an
artist? First of all, there are the "aliveness" and scope of his writing.
At its best, Tolstoy's prose conveys a thrilling immediacy within vast
dimensions—a vital yet varied sensitivity to life. And this is what
Isaiah Berlin describes as his foxlike achievement:

No one has ever excelled Tolstoy in expressing the specific flavour, the exact
quality of a feeling . . . the inner and outer texture and 'feel' of a look, a
thought, a pang of sentiment, no less than that of the specific pattern of a
situation, or an entire period, continuous segments of lives of individuals,
families, communities, entire nations. The celebrated life-likeness of every
object and every person in his world derives from this astonishing capacity of
presenting every ingredient of it in its fullest individual essence. . . .[10]

This effect of almost startling immediacy may be related to Tolstoy's
keen sensibilities, to his empathy with every person upon the earth,
every animal, even every plant and fragment of the planet's crust. In a
more technical sense, the vividness of his writing owes much to three
literary techniques: so-called "body language," inner monologue, and
"making strange." This last method, sometimes called defamiliariza-
tion, is put to particularly graphic and satirical use in Tolstoy's story
"Strider," in which a horse describes people to other horses. These
beings, the horse declares, actually use the expression "my horse,"

which seems as strange to him as saying "my land," "my water," and "my air" (12:24). What is more, the horse reports, there are men who speak of a woman as their own, even though she mates with other men. These beings, he concludes, strive not so much to do what is good in life as to call as many things as possible "my own." In its most extreme form, the technique of making strange might be used in depicting reality through the eyes of an alien observer reporting on the odd creatures who inhabit the planet earth, which Tolstoy almost did in his story "Razrushenie ada i vosstanovlenie ego" ("The Destruction of Hell and Its Restoration," 1903). The chief Devil, returning to earth hundreds of years after Christ's death, is astonished and delighted to find that evil still abounds: people are now perverted by something called "the church," which teaches that its ritual of consuming bread and wine is "very useful for saving one's soul" (12:396). When people arrive in Hell, they are "very surprised" that this has failed to save them.

Tolstoy's art is also remarkable for its power, delicacy, and freshness. Upon learning that Turgenev had likened Tolstoy to an "elephant" in the greatness of his talent, Konstantin Leontev was pleased to agree: "It is well known that an elephant can easily lift a large log with his trunk and cast it aside as well as carefully lift a butterfly from a flower."[11] And in 1891, Chekhov wrote to an associate that every night he would wake up and read *War and Peace:* "One reads with such curiosity and such naive astonishment as though one had never read before."[12]

Not long before his death, Tolstoy made the now famous remark, "When I was writing *Childhood,* it seemed to me that no one before me had yet so felt and depicted all the charm and poetry of childhood."[13] The English word *charm* may be old-fashioned, but this quality of Tolstoy's writing may never seem dated. From little Nicholas Irtenyev's magically ambitious attempt to draw a hunting scene entirely in blue, the only color he had, through young Natasha's innocent joy in spying on a kiss in the conservatory (*War and Peace*), and of course her life-affirming rapture at the impatiently moon-splashed night, to the beautiful but doomed reunion in *Anna Karenina* as Seryozha, trying to prolong this dream come true, cuddles warmly against his mother— the reader can only marvel, and feel somehow humbly, unashamedly naked.

Notes and References

Preface

    1. Iurii Olesha, *Povesti i rasskazy* (Tales and stories) (Moscow: Khudo-zhestvennaya literatura, 1965), 491.

Chapter One

    1. See Boris Eikhenbaum, *The Young Tolstoi,* trans. David Boucher et al (Ann Arbor, 1972), 10–11.
    2. Isaiah Berlin, *The Hedgehog and the Fox* (New York, 1970), 1–2.
    3. R. F. Christian, ed., *Tolstoy's Letters* (New York, 1978), 1:2, 12.
    4. Ernest J. Simmons, *Leo Tolstoy* (London, 1949), 30.
    5. Ibid., 36.
    6. Ibid., 62.
    7. Christian, ed., *Tolstoy's Letters,* 1:95.
    8. Ibid., 1:141.
    9. Ibid., 1:168.
    10. Ibid., 1:169.
    11. Boris Eikhenbaum, *Tolstoi in the Sixties,* trans. Duffield White (Ann Arbor, 1982), 108–11. See also Christian, ed., *Tolstoy's Letters,* 1:179.
    12. Christian, ed., *Tolstoy's Letters,* 1:221.
    13. Ibid., 1:202, 273.
    14. Ibid., 1:283.
    15. Ibid., 1:277.
    16. Simmons, *Leo Tolstoy,* 437.
    17. Christian, ed., *Tolstoy's Letters,* 2:399.
    18. Simmons, *Leo Tolstoy,* 473.
    19. Christian, ed., *Tolstoy's Letters,* 2:637.
    20. Simmons, *Leo Tolstoy,* 714–15.
    21. Ibid., 742.
    22. Ibid., 792.

Chapter Two

    1. Christian, ed., *Tolstoy's Letters,* 1:35.
    2. R. F. Christian, *Tolstoy: A Critical Introduction* (Cambridge, 1969), 23.
    3. Eikhenbaum, *The Young Tolstoi,* 62.
    4. A. V. Knowles, ed., *Tolstoy: The Critical Heritage* (London, 1978), 64.

5. Christian, *Tolstoy*, 27–31.

6. See Dmitri S. Merezhkovski, *Tolstoi as Man and Artist, with an Essay on Dostoevski* (Westport, Conn., 1970), 165–88.

7. Simmons, *Leo Tolstoy*, 155.

8. See Christian, ed., *Tolstoy's Letters*, 2:485.

9. See Alexander F. Zweers, *Grown-up Narrator and Childlike Hero: An Analysis of the Literary Devices Employed in Tolstoj's Trilogy Childhood, Boyhood and Youth* (The Hague, 1971), 51.

10. See Victor Shklovsky, "Art as Technique," in *Russian Formalist Criticism: Four Essays*, trans. Lee T. Lemon and Marion J. Reis (Lincoln, Neb.: University of Nebraska Press, 1965), 13–18.

11. Christian, *Tolstoy*, 33.

12. See my *Nabokov and Others: Patterns in Russian Literature* (Ann Arbor, Michigan: Ardis, 1979), 47–49.

13. Eikhenbaum, *Young Tolstoi*, 55.

14. See Zweers, *Grown-up Narrator*, 47–48.

15. George Steiner, *Tolstoy or Dostoevsky: An Essay in the Old Criticism* (New York, 1961), 270.

Chapter Three

1. Simmons, *Leo Tolstoy*, 156.

2. See Christian, *Tolstoy*, 95.

3. Ibid., 64–65.

4. See ibid., 70, and George Rapall Noyes, *Tolstoy* (New York, 1968), 50, respectively.

5. D. S. Mirsky, *A History of Russian Literature from its Beginnings to 1900* (New York: Random House, 1958), 269.

6. Christian, *Tolstoy*, 72.

Chapter Four

1. Christian, ed., *Tolstoy's Letters*, 1:206.

2. Ibid., 1:197.

3. Simmons, *Leo Tolstoy*, 309.

4. See Steiner, *Tolstoy or Dostoevsky*, 80.

5. Henry James, *The Tragic Muse* (New York: Charles Scribner's Sons, 1908), x.

6. L. N. Tolstoi, *Sobranie sochinenii v dvadsati dvukh tomakh* [Collected works in twenty-two volumes] (Moscow, 1978-), 7:356.

7. John Hagan, "A Pattern of Character Development in *War and Peace: Prince Andrej*," *Slavic and East European Journal* 13 no. 2 (Summer 1969): 165.

8. Käte Hamburger, "Tolstoy's Art," in Ralph E. Matlaw, ed., *Tolstoy: A Collection of Critical Essays* (Englewood Cliffs, N. J., 1967), 72.

9. Christian, *Tolstoy,* 120.

10. Steiner, *Tolstoy or Dostoevsky,* 118.

11. Hagan, "Pattern," 169.

12. Edward Wasiolek, *Tolstoy's Major Fiction* (Chicago, 1978), 83.

13. Ibid., 105.

14. See Matlaw, ed., *Tolstoy: A Collection of Critical Essays,* 3.

15. Hagan, "Pattern," 189.

16. Ruth Crego Benson, *Women in Tolstoy: The Ideal and the Erotic* (Urbana, 1973), ix.

17. Barbara Heldt Monter, "Tolstoj's Path Towards Feminism," in Victor Terras, ed., *American Contributions to the Eighth International Congress of Slavists* (Columbus, Ohio: Slavica, 1978), 2:529.

18. Atkinson et al., eds., *Women in Russia* (Stanford, Calif.: Stanford University Press, 1977), 15–16.

19. Henri Troyat, *Tolstoy,* trans. Nancy Amphoux (New York, 1967), 322.

20. Dmitri Pisarev, "The Old Gentry," in George Gibian, trans., Norton Critical Edition of *War and Peace* (New York, 1966), 1378–79.

21. See Vytas Dukas and Glenn A. Sandstrom, "Taoistic Patterns in *War and Peace,*" *Slavic and East European Journal* 14, no. 2 (Summer 1970):185.

22. Ibid., 190.

23. Frank Seeley, "Tolstoy's Philosophy of History," in Malcolm Jones, ed., *New Essays on Tolstoy* (Cambridge, 1978), 182.

24. Alexander Pushkin, *Eugene Onegin,* trans. Vladimir Nabokov (Princeton, 1975) 1:268.

25. Christian, *Tolstoy,* 100.

26. R. F. Christian, *Tolstoy's "War and Peace"* (Oxford, 1968), 106–7.

27. Paul Debreczeny, "Freedom and Necessity: A Reconsideration of *War and Peace,*" *Papers on Language and Literature,* Spring 1971, 185.

28. F. M. Dostoevskii, *Sobranie sochinenii* [Collected works], 10 vols. (Moscow: Goslitizdat, 1956–58), 6:25.

Chapter Five

1. Simmons, *Leo Tolstoy,* 340.

2. W. Gareth Jones, "George Eliot's *Adam Bede* and Tolstoy's Conception of *Anna Karenina,*" *Modern Language Review* 61 (1966):473–81.

3. Boris Eikhenbaum, *Tolstoi in the Seventies,* trans. Albert Kaspin (Ann Arbor, 1982), 137.

4. Christian, ed., *Tolstoy's Letters,* 1:271.

5. Christian, *Tolstoy,* 169–70.

6. Christian, ed., *Tolstoy's Letters,* 1:311.

7. Ibid., 1:296.

8. Sydney Schultze, *The Structure of "Anna Karenina"* (Ann Arbor, 1982), 18–23.

9. Ibid., 24.

10. Elisabeth Stenbock-Fermor, *The Architecture of "Anna Karenina"* (Lisse, Belgium, 1975), 26, 100. See also pp. 45–46 for an ingenious discussion of the theme of Anna's "book and candle."

11. Schultze, *Structure,* 114.

12. Ibid., 151–52.

13. John Bayley, *Tolstoy and the Novel* (New York, 1967), 174.

14. Eikhenbaum, *Tolstoi in the Seventies,* 137–43.

15. Vladimir Nabokov, *Lectures on Russian Literature,* ed. Fredson Bowers (New York, 1981), 146–47.

16. Ibid., 137.

17. See Christian, *Tolstoy,* 169.

18. Christian, ed., *Tolstoy's Letters,* 1:202.

19. Steiner, *Tolstoy or Dostoevsky,* 67.

20. Christian, ed., *Tolstoy's Letters,* 1:97.

21. See Schultze, *Structure,* 118–22.

22. See Konstantin Leont'ev, *Analiz, stil' i veianie* [Analysis, style and atmosphere] (1911; reprint, Providence, 1965), 72–73.

23. Schultze, *Structure,* 124.

24. Merezhkovski, *Tolstoi,* 216–20.

25. Eikhenbaum, *Tolstoi in the Seventies,* 161.

26. Schultze, *Structure,* 116–17.

27. A. P. Chekhov, *Polnoe sobranie sochinenii* [Complete works], 30 vols. (Moscow: Nauka, 1974–82), 9:16.

28. See Christian, *Tolstoy's "War and Peace,"* 148–66, for an excellent discussion of Tolstoy's use of repetition.

29. See Schultze, *Structure,* 85–86.

30. Christian, ed., *Tolstoy's Letters,* 1:296.

31. Schultze, *Structure,* 131.

32. Ibid., 124.

33. Ibid., 112.

34. Christian, ed., *Tolstoy's Letters,* 1:123.

35. See Schultze, *Structure,* 115.

36. See ibid., 112–13.

37. See ibid., 110–11.

38. News item in *Tula Province News,* 1872. See the Norton Critical Edition of *Anna Karenina* (New York, 1970), 745.

Chapter Six

1. Knowles, *Tolstoy: The Critical Heritage,* 32.

2. Christian, ed., *Tolstoy's Letters,* 1:222.

3. Bayley, *Tolstoy and the Novel,* 192.

4. Christian, ed., *Tolstoy's Letters,* 2:667.

5. Ibid., 2:478.

6. Wasiolek, *Tolstoy's Major Fiction,* 163.

7. Albert Cook, "The Moral Vision: Tolstoy," in Matlaw, ed., *Tolstoy: A Collection of Critical Essays,* 126.

8. See Dorothy Green, *"The Kreutzer Sonata:* Tolstoy and Beethoven," *Melbourne Slavonic Studies* 1 (1967); Green's argument is summarized by R. F. Christian, *Tolstoy,* 232–33.

9. Tolstoy, 10:533.

10. Ibid., 3:468.

11. Simmons, *Leo Tolstoy,* 197.

12. Christian, ed., *Tolstoy's Letters,* 1:122.

13. Christian, *Tolstoy,* 89.

14. Wasiolek, *Tolstoy's Major Fiction,* 33.

15. L. N. Tolstoi, *Polnoe sobranie sochinenii v 90-kh tomakh* [Complete works in 90 volumes] (Moscow, 1928–58), 5:301.

16. Eikhenbaum, *Young Tolstoi,* 10.

17. Christian, *Tolstoy,* 237.

18. See Boris Sorokin, "Ivan Il'ich as Jonah: A Cruel Joke," *Canadian Slavic Studies* 5, no. 4 (Winter 1971):503.

19. Matlaw, ed., *Tolstoy: A Collection of Critical Essays,* 6.

20. See E. W. Trahan, "Tolstoy's 'Master and Man'—A Symbolic Narrative," *Slavic and East European Journal* 7, no. 3 (Fall 1963):258–68.

21. L. N. Tolstoi, *Sobranie sochinenii v dvadsati dvukh tomakh,* 12:474.

22. Bayley, *Tolstoy and the Novel,* 95.

23. Christian, ed., *Tolstoy's Letters,* 2:490–91.

Chapter Seven

1. Simmons, *Leo Tolstoy,* 628–29.

2. Ibid., 605.

3. Ibid., 629–30.

4. Christian, *Tolstoy,* 223–24.

5. Bayley, *Tolstoy and the Novel,* 248.

6. Steiner, *Tolstoy or Dostoevsky,* 92.

7. There were four appearances of this "serial character" in Tolstoy's works, and he had plans for a fifth one. See Mary F. Zirin, "Prince Dmitri Nekhlyudov: A Synthetic Portrait," *Russian Literature Triquarterly,* no. 17 (1982), 85, 100.

8. See Eikhenbaum, *Young Tolstoi,* 10–11.

9. Bayley, *Tolstoy and Novel,* 261.

10. Eikhenbaum, *Young Tolstoi,* 59.

11. Steiner, *Tolstoy or Dostoevsky,* 250, 284.

Chapter Eight

1. See Monter, 533.
2. The story was not original; see L. N. Tolstoi, *sobranie sochinenii v dvadsati dvukh tomakh*, 12:472.
3. Simmons, *Leo Tolstoy*, 132.
4. Berlin, *Hedgehog*, 2, 1.
5. S. Rozanova, ed., *L. N. Tolstoi: perepiska s russkimi pisateliami* [Tolstoy's correspondence with Russian writers] (Moscow: Gosudarstvennoe izdatel'stvo khudozhestvennoi literatury, 1962), 93.
6. Berlin, *Hedgehog*, 2, See also 41, 81.
7. Steiner, *Tolstoy or Dostoevsky*, 278.
8. Bayley, *Tolstoy and the Novel*, 95.
9. Christian, *Tolstoy*, 266.
10. Berlin, *Hedgehog*, 40.
11. Leont'ev, *Analiz*, 22, 25.
12. Chekhov, *Polnoe sobranie sochinenii*, 4:291.
13. Valentin Bulgakov, *L. N. Tolstoi v poslednii god ego zhizni* [The Last year of L. N. Tolstoy] (Moscow, 1960), 162.

Selected Bibliography

PRIMARY SOURCES

Sobranie sochinenii v dvadtsati dvukh tomakh (Collected works in 22 volumes). Moscow: Khudozhestvennaia literatura, 1978–. At the time of writing, publication is still in progress, having reached volume 17.

Polnoe sobranie sochinenii v 90-kh tomakh (Complete works in 90 volumes) Moscow: Khudozhestvennaia literatura, 1928–58.

The standard English translations are by Louise and Aylmer Maude. *The Centenary Edition of Tolstoy.* 21 vols. London: Oxford University Press, 1929–37. The Maude translations are also available in the Norton Critical Editions of *War and Peace* (New York, 1966) and *Anna Karenina* (New York, 1970), both edited by George Gibian, and in *Great Short Works of Leo Tolstoy* (New York: Harper & Row, 1967), with an introduction by John Bayley.

Childhood, Boyhood, and Youth. Translated by Alexandra and Sverre Lyngstad. New York: Washington Square Press, 1968.

Resurrection is available in a restored version of the Louise Maude translation by John W. Strahan, New York: Washington Square Press, 1963.

The Portable Tolstoy. New York: Penguin books, 1978, provides a useful selection of short works, including Tolstoy's *Confession,* as well as excerpts from longer works, including *What Is Art?,* with an introductory essay by John Bayley.

Tolstoy's Letters. 2 vols. New York: Charles Scribner's Sons, 1978, provides an excellent translation by R. F. Christian of 608 of Tolstoy's 8,500 published letters, with informative notes and introductory essays.

SECONDARY SOURCES

1. Bibliographical Aids

Egan, David R., and Melinda A. Egan. *Leo Tolstoy: An Annotated Bibliography of English-Language Sources to 1978.* Metuchen, N. J.: Scarecrow Press, 1979. Very useful, very comprehensive.

Knowles, A. V. ed. *Tolstoy: The Critical Heritage.* London: Routledge & Kegan Paul, 1978. A chronological selection of early critical reactions to Tolstoy's works, mainly his fiction.

Shelyapina, N. G. et al., ed. *Bibliografiia literatury o Tolstom* (Bibliography of literature about Tolstoy) *1917–58, 1959–61,* and *1962–67.* 3 vols. Moscow: Kniga, 1960, 1965, 1972. Limited to works published in the Soviet Union, some quite unimportant.

Sorokin, Boris. *Tolstoy in Prerevolutionary Russian Criticism.* Columbus: Ohio State University Press, 1979. Organized according to types of critics, for example, radical, aesthetic, symbolist, etc.

Terry, Garth M. *East European Languages and Literatures: A Subject and Name Index to Articles in English-Language Journals, 1900–1977.* Santa Barbara, Calif.: Clio Press, 1978. Lists several hundred articles, organized as to Tolstoy's individual works, Tolstoy in general, and Tolstoy and other major figures.

Wasiolek, Edward. *Tolstoy's Major Fiction.* Chicago: University of Chicago Press, 1978. Contains a 25-page annotated bibliography.

2. Biographical and Critical Works

Asquith, Cynthia. *Married to Tolstoy.* Boston: Houghton Mifflin, 1961. Sympathetic account of the difficulties and contributions of Countess Tolstoy.

Bayley, John. *Tolstoy and the Novel.* London: Chatto & Windus, 1966. Valuable study of Tolstoy's major works; emphasizes *War and Peace.*

Benson, Ruth C. *Women in Tolstoy: The Ideal and the Erotic.* Chicago: University of Illinois Press, 1973. Explores Tolstoy's ambivalent attitude toward women.

Berlin, Isaiah. *The Hedgehog and the Fox: An Essay on Tolstoy's View of History.* New York: Simon & Schuster, 1953. Provocative, landmark interpretation of Tolstoy as "knowing many things" but trying to discover the One Truth.

Bulgakov, Valentin F. *The Last Year of Leo Tolstoy.* Translated by Ann Dunnigan. New York: Dial, 1971. An informative account by his male secretary of Tolstoy's last struggles, crises, and opinions.

Christian, R. F. *Tolstoy: A Critical Introduction.* Cambridge: Cambridge University Press, 1969. Concise, informative, very useful.

———— *Tolstoy's "War and Peace," A Study.* Oxford: Clarendon Press, 1962. Detailed examination of the novel's evolution, plus a careful analysis of its characterizations, structure, and style.

Eikhenbaum, Boris. *The Young Tolstoi.* Translated by David Boucher et al. Ann Arbor, Mich.: Ardis, 1972. Classic analysis of Tolstoy's early works.

———— *Tolstoi in the Sixties.* Translated by Duffield White. Ann Arbor, Mich.: Ardis, 1982. Centerpiece volume of the best study of Tolstoy in any language.

———— *Tolstoi in the Seventies.* Translated by Albert Kaspin. Ann Arbor, Mich.: Ardis, 1982. Classic, comprehensive study of the decade of *Anna Karenina.*

Ermilov, V. *Tolstoi romanist* (Tolstoy the novelist). Moscow: Khudozhestvennaia literatura, 1965. Study of Tolstoy's three major novels by a Soviet critic.

Fodor, Alexander. *Tolstoy and the Russians.* Ann Arbor, Mich.: Ardis, 1984. Traces the significance of Tolstoy for Russians to the present; useful biographical notes appended.

Gibian, George. *Tolstoy and Shakespeare.* The Hague: Mouton, 1957. Valuable analysis of Tolstoy's antipathy toward Shakespeare.

Gifford, Henry. *Tolstoy.* Oxford and New York: Oxford University Press, 1982. Perceptive discussion of Tolstoy's thought as embodied in his writings.

Goldenweizer, A. B. *Talks with Tolstoy.* Translated by S. Koteliansky. New York: Horizon, 1969. Conversations on a wide range of topics from homelife to philosophy with Tolstoy's musician friend.

Gorky, Maxim. *Reminiscences of L. N. Tolstoy.* Translated by S. S. Koteliansky and L. Woolf. New York: B. W. Huebsch, 1920. Insightful recollections.

Green, Martin. *Tolstoy and Gandhi, Men of Peace.* New York: Basic Books, 1983. Side by side examination of the two men's lives, emphasizing their later-life responses to historical forces.

Jones, Malcolm, ed. *New Essays on Tolstoy.* Cambridge: Cambridge University Press, 1978. Useful essays by British scholars; bibliographical survey in Great Britain appended.

Lavrin, Janko. *Tolstoy: An Approach.* 1946. Reprint. New York: Russell & Russell, 1968. Discusses Tolstoy's personality and writings, emphasizing his preference for precivilized group consciousness.

Leont'ev, Konstantin. *O romanakh gr. L. N. Tolstogo. Analiz, stil' i veianie* (On Tolstoy's novels. Analysis, style and atmosphere). 1911. Reprint. Providence, R. I.: Brown, 1965. Perceptive analysis; both subtle and provocative.

Matlaw, Ralph E, ed. *Tolstoy: A Collection of Critical Essays.* Englewood Cliffs, N.J.: Prentice Hall, 1967. Very fine selection of articles.

Maude, Aylmer *The Life of Tolstoy.* 2 vols. London: Oxford, 1930. Still the best biography of Tolstoy in English.

Merezhkovski, Dmitri S. *Tolstoi as Man and Artist, with an Essay on Dostoevski.* 1902. Reprint. Westport, Conn.: Greenwood, 1970. Well known for its discussion of Tolstoy's use of "body language."

Noyes, George R. *Tolstoy.* 1918. Reprint. New York: Dover, 1968. A study of Tolstoy's major works, demonstrating their interrelationship with his life.

Opul'skaia, L., and **S. Rozanova,** eds. *L. N. Tolstoi v vospominaniiakh sovremennikov* (Tolstoy in the memoirs of his contemporaries). 2 vols. Moscow: Goslitizdat, 1960. The wide range of authors includes Bunin, Gorky, Stanislavsky, and Leonid Pasternak.

Redpath, Theodore. *Tolstoy*. London: Bowes & Bowes, 1969. Concise, clearly organized survey of Tolstoy's ideas, works, and life.

Rolland, Romain. *Tolstoy*. Translated by Bernard Miall. New York: E. P. Dutton, 1911. Enthusiastic, perceptive early study of Tolstoy's works and life.

Schultze, Sydney. *The Structure of "Anna Karenina."* Ann Arbor, Mich.: Ardis, 1982. An excellent, comprehensive analysis of the novel.

Simmons, Ernest J. *Leo Tolstoy*. 2 vols. Boston: Little, Brown, 1946. The best analysis in English of Tolstoy's life and works.

———— *Introduction to Tolstoy's Writings*. Chicago: University of Chicago Press, 1968. Concise, informative; concludes with a chapter on "Tolstoy's Image Today."

Steiner, George. *Tolstoy or Dostoevsky: An Essay in the Old Criticism*. New York: Random House, 1959. A brilliant study with many challenging insights.

Stenbock-Fermor, Elisabeth. *The Architecture of "Anna Karenina."* Lisse, Belgium: Peter De Ridder Press, 1975. Both useful and ingenious.

Tolstoy, Alexandra. *Tolstoy: A Life of My Father*. Translated by E. R. Hapgood. New York: Harper, 1953. Sympathetic, detailed biography emphasizing family relationships.

Troyat, Henri. *Tolstoy*. Translated by Nancy Amphoux. New York: Doubleday, 1969. A colorful and somewhat unscholarly account of Tolstoy's turbulent life, drawing upon his autobiographical works.

Wasiolek, Edward. *Tolstoy's Major Fiction*. Chicago: University of Chicago Press, 1978. A stimulating study with some fresh, controversial insights.

Zweers, Alexander F. *Grown-up Narrator and Childlike Hero: An Analysis of the Literary Devices Employed in Tolstoj's Trilogy Childhood, Boyhood and Youth*. The Hague: Mouton, 1971. Helpful analysis, plus a survey of criticism of Tolstoy's trilogy.

Index

DATE DUE
